BABIES
DON'T MAKE
SMALL TALK
(SO WHY
SHOULD I?)

BABIES DON'T MAKE SMALL TALK (SO WHY SHOULD I?)

The Introvert's Guide to Surviving Parenthood

JULIE VICK

The Countryman Press
A Division of W. W. Norton & Company
Independent Publishers Since 1923

Copyright © 2021 by Julie Vick

"30 Totally Ridiculous Reasons Your Baby Isn't Sleeping" first appeared in *Parents* magazine.

"Children's Birthday Party Survival Prep List" is adapted from an article that first appeared in *Razed* as "A Kids' Birthday Party Screening Questionnaire for Introverts."

All rights reserved
Printed in the United States of America

For information about permission to reproduce selections from this book, write to Permissions, The Countryman Press, 500 Fifth Avenue, New York, NY 10110

For information about special discounts for bulk purchases, please contact W. W. Norton Special Sales at specialsales@wwnorton.com or 800-233-4830

Manufacturing by LSC Communications, Harrisonburg
Book design by Chris Welch Design
Production manager: Devon Zahn

Library of Congress Cataloging-in-Publication Data

Names: Vick, Julie, author.
Title: Babies don't make small talk (so why should I?) : the introvert's guide to surviving parenthood / Julie Vick.
Description: New York, NY : The Countryman Press, a division of W.W. Norton & Company, Inc., [2021] | Includes index.
Identifiers: LCCN 2021014294 | ISBN 9781682686553 (hardcover) | ISBN 9781682686560 (epub)
Subjects: LCSH: Parenting—Humor. | Child rearing—Humor. | Introverts—Humor. | Introversion—Humor.
Classification: LCC HQ769 V523 2021 | DDC 649/.1220207—dc23
LC record available at https://lccn.loc.gov/2021014294

The Countryman Press
www.countrymanpress.com

A division of W. W. Norton & Company, Inc.
500 Fifth Avenue, New York, NY 10110
www.wwnorton.com

10 9 8 7 6 5 4 3 2 1

FOR DAVE, GRAHAM, AND BECK.

CONTENTS

Introduction   xi

PART ONE
YOUR LAST TASTES OF FREEDOM

1. To Have or Not to Have a Kid   3

2. Pregnancy: When a Baby Is Going to Come
   Out of Your Body (One Way or Another)   10

3. Expecting Another Way   24

4. Sharing the News   28

5. Panic! at the Baby Shower   34

6. If You Overthink Things and You Know It:
   Selecting a Baby Name   41

PART TWO
SURVIVING THE FIRST YEAR

7. Showtime: The Birth   51

8. Social Overload: Managing Well-Meaning Friends and Family   59

9. Nourishment with a Dash of Judgement: Feeding Your Baby   65

10. Not Even Alone in Your Sleep: Managing Lack of Sleep   70

11. Information Overload: Dealing with Social Media and Conflicting Advice   76

12. I Might Actually Be Here to Make Friends: Finding Parent Friends   81

13. Securing Your Alone Time: Selecting Childcare   90

14. Required Outings: Managing Doctor Visits   99

15. How to Deal with Never Being Alone   104

16. The Days Are Long, but the Baby Classes Are Longer: Surviving Parent-Child Classes   111

17. Birthday Parties: Throwing Them   115

PART THREE
WELCOME TO TODDLERVILLE

18. Forced Socialization: Playdates   121

19. Attending Kids' Birthday Parties   127

20. All Eyes on You: Public Tantrums   133

21. Kids Are Loud: Trying to Find Your Quiet   139

22. Bedtime Struggles   144

23. The Great Outdoors: How to Survive the Playground   149

24. Food Fights: Eating Out with Your Toddler   155

25. I Need You! Dealing with Constant Interruptions   162

26. Babes in Travel Land: Traveling with Young Kids   166

27. Welcome to the Jungle: Starting Preschool   173

28. The More the Scarier: Expecting Another Child   178

29. Reflection Time   182

Acknowledgments   188

Index   189

INTRODUCTION

I have always been an overthinker, so when it came time to consider parenting, I was overwhelmed by all the choices—first with the question of whether or not to have a kid, then with the decision of when to start trying for one. Pregnancy brought on a new round of decisions—could I eat some sushi if it was cooked? Which people should I tell the news to and when? Should I risk running baby names by anyone or guard them like the contents of a teenager's diary? The social aspect of parenting was also a big adjustment for me. On the one hand, having a baby makes for a pretty good excuse to turn down an invitation to an awkward dinner party. On the other hand, parenting thrusts you into an array of playdates, park interactions, and birthday parties, which can be overwhelming when social interactions leave you feeling drained.

I've also always needed alone time to recharge, and

becoming a parent meant I was suddenly with another tiny person during most of my waking and some of my sleeping hours. While said tiny person won't force you to engage in banal small talk about the weather, they are almost always within chatting distance. A baby can make it difficult for you to do something as simple as go to the grocery store alone.

People like me often identify as introverts, although the exact definition of introversion can vary. In broad terms, introverts draw energy from alone time and an inner world, whereas extroverts draw energy from social situations and the external world.* People who are somewhere in the middle are ambiverts. I teach at the college level (something that has taken me a while to get more comfortable with), and while I enjoy teaching and interacting with students, after a class I often feel drained and in need of time to recharge. I once chatted with an acquaintance at a small party about teaching (this was before I had kids, when I had a lot fewer excuses for avoiding parties). "Don't you just walk out of the room completely energized after a class?" he asked. That's the difference between an extrovert and an introvert. At the party, I just stumbled through some awkward response to the guy and then probably made an excuse to head home, since I could check off "accomplished some socializing" on my mental to-do list.

---

* The Myers & Briggs Foundation, "Extraversion or Introversion": www.myersbriggs.org/my-mbti-personality-type/mbti-basics/extraversion-or-introversion.htm.

I'M NOT HERE TO MAKE SMALL TALK: CHARACTERISTICS OF INTROVERTS

Since the world often feels built for people who aren't exhausted by the thought of attending a networking mixer, discovering you are an introvert can be a relief. You don't feel weird for avoiding team projects or for feeling relieved when some plans are canceled—you have a legitimate personality type! Susan Cain's excellent book *Quiet: The Power of Introverts in a World That Can't Stop Talking* discusses introversion in great detail. The book identifies some common characteristics of introverts, including that they often:

- Prefer less external stimulation (are more comfortable in quieter spaces or socializing in smaller groups)
- Enjoy solitude
- Dislike conflict
- Prefer listening to talking, and tend to think before they speak
- Prefer deep discussions to small talk

Introverts are good listeners, make good friends, and enjoy discussing subjects that interest them. But living an involved inner life can lead to a lot of overthinking and second-guessing. And since raising children is not exactly a quiet and conflict-free existence, becoming a parent can pose just a few small hurdles to introverts.

REASONS BESIDES INTROVERSION WHY YOU MAY AVOID SMALL TALK

Introversion is different from shyness (feeling awkward or worried during social situations)*, and extreme discomfort and fear in social situations can sometimes be a condition known as social anxiety disorder.† Some people (like me) are both shy and introverted—having to attend a birth class full of people I didn't know made me both anxious (Who will be there? Will I be called on to answer questions? Will I have to role-play something?) and drained of energy afterward. Shy extroverts may feel worried they will say something awkward during the class but may be energized by the social interaction when it's over. Outgoing extroverts are the ones volunteering to act out a birthing position in front of the class and trying to get all their newfound friends to meet up for dinner when it's over. I'm guessing that last one does not describe you, but if it does, welcome, and thank you for being willing to draw attention away from the rest of us at times.

There are some people who have personality traits that can have some overlap with introversion, like highly sensitive people or empaths. If you are unsure whether you

---

* American Psychological Association, "Shyness," www.apa.org/topics/shyness.

† National Institute of Mental Health, "Social Anxiety Disorder: More Than Just Shyness," www.nimh.nih.gov/health/publications/social-anxiety-disorder-more-than-just-shyness/index.shtml.

are any or all of these, there are several internet rabbit holes of explanations and Buzzfeed quizzes just waiting for you to search them out.

PANDEMIC PARENTING

The COVID-19 pandemic coincided with me writing this book. Hopefully you are reading this from some point in a utopian future in which the pandemic has ended and everything has been overhauled so that the world has a cornucopia of emergency childcare options and magical trees that grow packages of toilet paper. But I realize there is a slight chance that may not be the case.

When stay-at-home orders first started in my area, in a lot of ways it felt like a return to the newborn stage of parenting to me—sleep and leaving the house were difficult, and there was a great deal of uncertainty about what was ahead. As an introverted parent, I was initially kind of relieved that my schedule was suddenly clear and that virtual happy hours and playdates were now possibilities—I could socialize without leaving my house or changing out of my pajamas. But as the weeks wore on, it became apparent that Zoom calls could get tiresome, and I began to miss in-person time with close friends. On the upside, the recent shift to more virtual socializing may be easier for some introverted parents, and it's something that I suspect may continue as an option after the pandemic is over.

IS THIS BOOK FOR ME?

So, who is this book for? You need not be a card-carrying introvert. (Besides, the cards are sometimes hard to acquire because no one wants to meet in person to hand them out.) You might be an introvert only in certain situations, or you might consider yourself more socially awkward or anxious than introverted. You'll probably find the content of the book more interesting if you are a parent or are on the road to parenthood, but if you have recently taken up an interest in reading about parenthood for some other reason, that's okay too. This book might be for you if some of the following statements sound familiar:

- You often let your phone calls go to voice mail and then text people back.
- You're still thinking about the time two years ago when a server said, "Enjoy your dinner," and you replied, "You too."
- The thought of hosting a party makes you anxious.
- The thought of attending a party makes you anxious.
- The thought of you being the center of attention at a party where you must wear a crown made of diapers kind of terrifies you.
- You've been told you are quiet, shy, or you should "come out of your shell" like you are some sort of ocean-dwelling mollusk.
- You'd prefer not to be overscheduled and are sometimes relieved when plans are canceled.

- Whenever you attend a networking event, big holiday gathering, or particularly rowdy knitting circle meetup, you need some downtime at home afterward.
- You are preparing for parenthood like it's coursework for a PhD by reading every book and website on the subject you can get your hands on.
- Some of the rest of the statements on this list apply to a friend or loved one, and you are trying to understand why they spend so much time hiding in the bathroom.

But most of all, this book is for people looking for some comic relief. Parenting is hard; sometimes laughter can help.

PART ONE

YOUR LAST TASTES
OF FREEDOM

1

To Have or Not to Have a Kid

Congratulations! If you are reading this, you must be considering having a kid. You are probably overanalyzing the pros and cons of this important decision. Or perhaps you're unexpectedly expecting and now freaking out. If it's the latter, this chapter may not provide you with a lot of assurances. There is no shame in just proceeding directly to chapter 2 now—no one will ever know.

The problem with the "Should you have kids?" question is that there is no one right answer for everyone. Maybe you're like some people who have always known that they wanted to have kids—in the same way that you've always known your greatest fear would be going door to door to sell a life-changing cleaning supply system. Other people don't really know if they want kids, or they think they do but have read one too many accounts of how difficult parenting is and are starting to have some doubts.

The type of child that you wind up with also varies widely—it's possible to have anywhere between one and eight babies at once, and the personality type of your new bundle of joy(s) could range from "potted plant" to "screams all day and much of the night." But it's a decision that needs to be made, so this chapter will discuss it.

I was always pretty sure I would eventually want to have kids, but not 100 percent sure. (To be fair, as an overthinker, I'm rarely 100 percent sure of anything.) I knew that kids were expensive and time-consuming and widely variable, and the studies saying that parents were less happy than their childless peers concerned me. I had done some babysitting as a teenager, but it mostly just stressed me out—the main draw was making enough money to be able to buy my own candy and hide it around my room like Claudia in The Baby-Sitters Club. I also was not one of those people who felt a deep need for a baby. Babies were cute and all, but I didn't really need to hold them (although I did end up awkwardly holding a lot of them because that is what some people want you to do when they have a baby). So I read a million things about having kids and had a lot of discussions with my husband and then ultimately decided it was worth going for. If you are reading this book as part of your self-assigned reading list on the topic of whether or not to have kids, welcome. I'm not sure it will help you make a decision, but I really appreciate your approach to making a decision by overloading yourself with information.

Before I had a kid, I really wanted to figure out what it would be like to have one. When possible, I like to observe things before jumping into them. So, in an ideal world, there would be a time machine that would allow me to pop into my future life as a parent to get a sense of what it was like exactly. But since no such machine has been invented (yet), I had to just make due with a lot of pros-and-cons lists, and also try to see what parenting was like by observing other people. Of course, people who have kids sometimes like to gloss over the difficulties of parenthood because if they are too honest they may scare you off altogether.

Still, there are some approximations for parenting that you can think about when trying to decide about having kids. The following pros-and-cons list contains some items for you to consider in the "should I be in charge of small children" department, followed by some blank space for you to fill in your own dreams/fears.

Pros-and-Cons List for Having Kids	
Pros	**Cons**
People will stop asking you when you are going to have kids.	People will start asking you about the specifics of your baby's sleep patterns and proficiency level with baby sign language.
Can dress someone other than your pets in cute Halloween costumes and snowsuits.	Possibility that kid will refuse to wear cute Halloween costume/snowsuit you have selected.
Good excuse not to have to attend your friend's experimental local theater production for 10 to 20 years.	Attending baby gym and music classes requires a lot of socializing and listening to loud music.

Pros	Cons
🍼 Your kid is a new possible candidate for caring for you when you're old.	🍼 Your kid may not actually care for you when you're old.
🍼 New excellent excuse to leave parties after two minutes.	🍼 You will get less sleep for the next 5 to 20 years.
🍼 Your previously dreaded commute will transform into cherished alone time.	🍼 Getting alone time will become much more difficult.
🍼 Life-changing love or whatever.	🍼 You will be invited to approximately 50 kids' birthday parties a year and will probably need to attend some of them.
🍼 Fill in your own:	🍼 Fill in your own:
_____	_____
_____	_____
_____	_____
_____	_____
_____	_____
_____	_____

PARENTAL READINESS CHALLENGES

Did the pros-and-cons list not help you decide how to make one of the most important decisions of your life? Strange. If you feel like you need a little more help figuring it out, then perhaps you should try something less abstract.

You can't really ever prepare for what it's like to become a parent, but you can probably hit the notes of some of the emotions. Try these simple tests to simulate real-life parenting challenges:

- Dine at a fast-food restaurant with a kids' play area at 5:30 p.m. on a Saturday night. How does this make you feel? Sad? Overwhelmed? Surprisingly happy because you have french fries?

- Borrow some goats from a farm and set them loose in your house while you cook three different meals. When you are done, feed each goat one bite of food and then throw the rest of the dinner in the trash. For a bonus challenge, pay a friend to come by your house to witness this spectacle and then tell you about how she only has to cook one thing for her goats and they always eat it, even if it's just kale and rusty tin cans.

- Do 100 loads of laundry and then watch a cute animal video a couple of times. Do these two things balance each other out?

- Set up your laptop on one end of a ping-pong table and set up a ping-pong robot on the other end. Turn on both the robot and your computer and then try to send some work emails. Could you focus? Did you manage to hit a few balls back?

- The night before an important work presentation, set your alarm to go off every hour on the hour throughout the night. Did you still make it to work? Did you even remember to give the presentation?

- Sign up for a parenting Facebook discussion group. Lurk around for a week and read the posts. If it seems pretty tame, just search for some past posts that include the words *circumcision, vaccination,* or *eating deli meat while pregnant.*

After you have completed the above challenges, find a friend or family member with kids and ask if you can visit their house on one or more of these occasions:

- After their kids are asleep
- On the morning of a holiday that involves receiving presents
- When they are reading a book you loved reading as a child

Once you've completed the challenges, reflect on the range of emotions you felt—did the good make up for the bad? Was the bad not really that bad? Do you feel totally ready to have a kid?

COMEBACKS TO NOSY QUESTIONS RELATED TO YOUR REPRODUCTION

For some reason, other people are very interested in if, when, and how you will be having children. When I got married, these questions started popping up with increasing frequency. There are plenty of reasons people do not want to discuss their procreation plans—they haven't decided yet, they've been struggling to conceive, they don't think the checkout line at the grocery store is the best time to talk about important life decisions. So here are some comebacks to questions that people really shouldn't be asking in the first place. You may not feel comfortable actually using them, but at least you can say them in your head:

"When are you going to have kids?"

What? You mean people still do that?

"Have you thought about freezing your eggs?"

No, I'm pretty sure that's not recommended. I just keep mine in the refrigerator.

"How many kids do you want to have?"

What's the world record these days? I'm just hoping to beat that.

"Just remember, you're not getting any younger."

Oh, actually, I am. I'm like Benjamin Button. I'm just going to wait it out until I turn into a baby myself and skip the whole labor thing.

"Hopefully my kids haven't scared you off from having your own kids."

[Just toss your head back and laugh maniacally.]

2

Pregnancy: When a Baby Is Going to Come Out of Your Body (One Way or Another)

 I've heard of people who loved being pregnant or say it was one of the happiest times in their lives. They were glowing! They were content! They weren't freaked out by how much their internal organs would get shoved around in nine months! But as a person who lives in her own head a lot, I found managing all the advice, anxieties, and diagrams about what would happen to my body exhausting at times. Sure, it is kind of amazing to be growing an actual human inside you, but it is less amazing when a stranger on the street guesses your due date to be in a couple weeks when you aren't even out of your second trimester yet.

Turns out, pregnancy is a magical journey involving plenty of opportunities for overthinking and awkward social situations. You may think that your baby is only the size of a poppy seed, but interactions around it will be the size of a coco de mer, which is actually a much larger type of seed. If your significant other is pregnant, you may be relieved not to be the focus of attention during this time, especially if the person carrying the baby doesn't really mind the attention. But you will still have to navigate telling (or not telling) people the news, others' opinions, and attending baby prep classes.

FUN FACT

The coco de mer is a type of palm tree nut that is roughly the size and shape of an inflatable neck pillow.

THE FIRST TRIMESTER

The first trimester can bring exhaustion, nausea, and, after spending too much time with Dr. Google, worry about something going wrong with the pregnancy. You may also have some bonus helpings of anxiety from previous losses or a lot of time spent trying to conceive. So your main mission in the first trimester is probably trying to avoid telling the entire world you are expecting.

Not to worry. Here is some guidance on navigating common situations that may give away your news before you are ready to do so.

The Alcohol Problem

One of the main reasons people will start to suspect you are pregnant is if you stop drinking alcohol—particularly if prior to getting pregnant you didn't pass up any chance to order a drink. If a spouse or partner also suddenly gives up alcohol in a show of solidarity, then you might as well have a blinking sign over your heads that says, BABY ON BOARD! If you had already abstained from alcohol prior to getting pregnant, kudos to you for dodging one of the first challenges of pregnancy.

Early in my first pregnancy, I attended a social event and did not have a drink in my hand. A friend tried to get me one and when I refused, she immediately asked if I was pregnant. If I were a better liar, I could have come up with some sort of convincing excuse on the spot, but I've always been an extremely bad liar, so I ended up just telling her before I really wanted to. By the time I was pregnant with my second child, I had grown wiser: When I had to attend a bachelorette party early in my pregnancy, I arrived at the bar early and ordered myself a mocktail I could sip (probably some sort of ginger ale drink since I was also dealing with a semi-constant state of nausea) and everyone just assumed it was a full-strength drink. Turns out a virgin mojito looks pretty much like a real mojito. So ordering a virgin drink out of earshot of your friends will help you avoid having to divulge any news until you are ready. If you do normally drink, try out some of these ways to avoid letting the news out before you are ready to reveal it:

- **Don't go out during the first trimester**: This may also raise some red flags, but you can just tell your friends you have a cold or are training for an Ironman Triathlon, so you are staying in for a while.

- **Order the drink:** Some friends will give you sidelong glances no matter what excuses you come up with, so just order a can of cheap beer and pretend to sip from it. If you have a friend or partner who is in the know, you can also just keep handing them your drink throughout the night. When I was pregnant, my husband and I would sometimes order the same type of beer and I would just hold mine. When he finished his beer, we would switch cans so I had the empty one.
- **Prepare excuses:** You can also just try going out and not ordering a drink, but you will need to come armed with an excuse. Maybe you aren't drinking because you are taking an antibiotic, or maybe you already had a bottle of tequila back at home.

The Sickness Problem

Another giveaway that someone might be "with child" is if they start racing off to the bathroom all the time or if they refuse to go to a coffee shop or on a tour of a sardine factory because of the smells. When I was pregnant, I spent most of the first trimester and part of the second one feeling sick. I had friends who never got sick at all and others who were throwing up for the duration of the nine months. If you're not lucky enough to avoid sickness, here are some strategies for dealing with this common problem:

- **Lie about having an illness:** Just say you are sick with something like food poisoning or the flu, or rely on the usefully vague "I'm just not feeling well."

- **Cancel plans:** Yes, it's annoying to be a chronic plan-canceler but the reality is that you may not be up for a night of clubbing in your first trimester. And since you have probably never really been up for a night of clubbing, now is the perfect time to give a polite "no" to some plans. When I was pregnant with my first son, I bowed out of some plans at the last minute when I was hit with a wave of nausea. I felt bad about doing this, but in the end, it wasn't a big deal.

- **Leave the country:** It will be hard for people to notice you are spending a lot of time in the bathroom when you are on a remote island in Finland. Sure, the people of Finland may ask you what's going on, but you will probably be more comfortable telling them the truth than admitting the news to your friends and family members.

The Busybody Problem

As I learned, some friends or family members will not hesitate to ask you if you are pregnant. You may already know who these people are because you have seen them grilling other friends on topics ranging from pregnancy to the details of their latest dermatologist appointment. The best option is to avoid them until you are ready to break the news via letter from your new house in Finland.

THE SECOND TRIMESTER

By the second trimester, you are hopefully feeling slightly better, but you will likely be faced with a new problem—your growing baby bump. Don't be fooled by those "I didn't know I was pregnant" shows where a petite woman never has any pregnancy symptoms for nine months and then one day just gives birth—most pregnant people do look like they are pregnant, and friends and strangers will notice. What's more, some people are compelled to touch pregnant bellies in the same way that others are compelled to pet cute dogs. You probably don't want this unwanted attention, and you would rather not make small talk with every stranger you meet on the street about when you are due and whether or not you should be drinking that decaf latte. Here are a few strategies to manage these problems:

- **Wear something distracting to draw people's eyes to another part of your body.** Perhaps a pair of neon yellow pants or a Kentucky derby hat.
- **Ask them questions before they have a chance to ask you.** If you notice someone staring at your belly, come up with a question about their life to distract them. Or just say "What's that?" and point behind them and then disappear when they turn around.

Ideas to Camouflage Your Belly

- **Choose extremely flowy clothes.** Perhaps instead of parachute pants just start wearing an actual parachute.

- **Stay seated.** It's harder to see the full size of someone's belly if they are always sitting down—so make a point to never stand up around your friends and family members.

- **Take up drumming.** Borrow a snare drum from your local high school marching band and start wearing it around your neck all the time. It will be hard for others to see that you are pregnant if you always have your drum with you.

THE THIRD TRIMESTER

By this point in your pregnancy, you probably will have revealed your news to most people (see chapter 4 for ideas on breaking the news). Now that that part is out of the way, you can focus your attention on prepping for the baby in other ways, like debating the merits of various baby names, choosing nursery decor, and braving a variety of pregnancy and birth classes.

MANAGING OTHERS' OPINIONS

Once you tell people you are expecting a baby or it becomes impossible to hide, you will begin to navigate a new world of questions and advice about what you should or shouldn't be doing while pregnant. Finding a trusted doctor or book to help you sort through the advice is useful (one that I found helpful was Emily Oster's book

Expecting Better). Nonexperts in your circle of family and friends will have opinions about what you should be eating, your birth plan, and whether you are allowed to wear a form-fitting dress or should just spend the next nine months in a muumuu. Some people can brush off such opinions, but if things that people say to you tend to get lodged in your brain for 5 to 20 years, then this sort of excessive commentary can be a problem.

When I was pregnant, I found that many people I encountered turned into pregnancy psychics. One friend predicted my baby would be bigger than average and another friend predicted he would be smaller than average (both my kids were about average when they were born). At a pedicure shop, a woman told me she thought I was having a boy because I was carrying low, and on a random street corner a woman asked me if I was due in a couple of weeks when I wasn't actually due for a couple of months. After I gave birth to my first son, I looked forward to no longer having people make comments about my stomach, but then a few months postpartum a child in the checkout line at Target pointed to my belly and said, "Baby!" I had to explain to her and her horrified mother that the baby had already come out, and then I immediately went home and threw the empire-waist shirt I was wearing in the trash. Still, there were some occasional perks to being visibly pregnant. One time, when I went into a convenience store to pay for my gas, the man behind the counter handed me a lollipop and said it was for the baby. So being pregnant can really be worth it when you start racking up free candy at 15 cents a pop.

WAYS TO AVOID AWKWARD CONVERSATIONS

Say, "Oh, I'm not pregnant." This one will work wonders for the stranger-on-the-street commentary, and it will hopefully have the added public service benefit of preventing said strangers from making comments to pregnant women they see in the future.

Headphones: Nothing says, "I can't hear what you are trying to say" like a pair of headphones. Don't go in for fancy ear buds that are hard for people to notice—get something much bigger. When you leave your house, people should assume you are on your way to a DJing gig.

Smile and nod: When a friend suggests that the only way to give birth is in an outdoor tub filled with French mineral water, just smile and nod and tell them you'll definitely look into that.

Pregnancy Message Board Questions

Q What is the best type of snack to eat while reading discussion fights on the expecting parent message board?

A Popcorn is a go-to, but really anything you have in the house will work.

Q Some guidelines say that you shouldn't eat any soft cheeses when you are pregnant, and other guidelines say that you can eat them as long as they are pasteurized. What should I do?

A Post this question to a pregnancy discussion board and then go make some popcorn.

MANAGING CLASSES

When you are expecting, there are a variety of classes offered in person and online to help you prepare for parenthood. I was not that big on the idea of attending classes where I might be called on to answer questions, but I saw the upsides to getting more information and maybe even connecting with other parents, so I signed up for some. Here are some options to consider.

Exercise Classes

If you already enjoyed a specific type of exercise prior to pregnancy, then you can likely continue to do it in some form while pregnant (although you might need to take a break if you are into extreme trampoline competitions or something). Or you can take this as an opportunity to try out new pregnancy exercises like water aerobics or speed walking through the grocery store while dodging passersby who have questions about when you are due.

On a more serious note, I sort of fell in love with prenatal yoga during my pregnancies. Prenatal yoga is one of my favorite types of yoga because it is extremely low-key. Can't hold downward dog for more than a second? No problem—you can take it easy. Break down in tears for some inexplicable reason halfway through? Everyone understands. Want to just lie on the floor with your eyes closed the whole time? Someone will just cover you up with one of the provided blankets and leave you alone. In the prenatal yoga classes that I took, we would often go around and briefly talk about how we were all doing at the beginning of each class. This sort of forced social sharing with strangers is usually the stuff of nightmares for me, but when I was pregnant it felt like a cheap form of therapy. I think part of the reason why I didn't mind it is that it wasn't mindless small talk—we were honestly discussing the highs and lows of pregnancy, a subject we were all pretty invested in. And discussing these things with a group of people I may never see again was somehow relaxing for me.

Baby Prep Classes

Prep classes are a mixed bag for the introvert. On the one hand, you probably want to learn everything possible about a given topic and be prepared for all outcomes. On the other, social events where you'll likely be expected to speak up can be draining. Still, my concern that I really did not know how to care for a newborn led me to sign up for some baby prep classes. There were a wide range to select from—from caring for a newborn 101 to a special class for expecting fathers. I didn't sign up for all the classes available, opting instead to read a lot of books and watch one video over and over again about how to swaddle a baby. (Spoiler alert: Swaddling a stuffed animal is *slightly* different than swaddling a real baby.) But my husband and I did take a baby safety class (which could have been subtitled "Learn about freak accidents to scar you for life from ever letting your child play with a bouncy ball"), and a breastfeeding class (which could have been subtitled "Come see a video about how far your nipples will be stretched out while feeding your baby!"). These classes were fine for me because they were brief and did not require any small group discussions. If you feel that you could benefit from some of the info in these classes, just opt for the ones that are on the shorter side and that don't require a lot of role-playing or breaking into groups. If the description of the class is not very detailed, reading online reviews of prior classes may help you sort out what is a good fit for you.

Birth Classes

This is one of the tougher choices (see previous section: Baby Prep Classes). It's probably something you want to take, but it's bound to get intimate and intimidating, and the only thing you may have in common with other attendees is that you are procreating. You could skip the class altogether, or just glean advice from the 500 books on pregnancy you are already reading, but you may pick up a helpful tip or two at the class. If you can get a recommendation from a like-minded friend about a class they did not hate, do. Otherwise, ~~call~~ send an email to the place running the class and ask for a detailed breakdown of what will occur during it. Look for a class that aligns with your birth plans and doesn't make you do some sort of weird acting out of a birth scene. If the people running the class refuse to reveal any details about what will happen in the class, then run fast the other way. Some classes may also be offered virtually, which is an option worth considering because you can always pretend your internet connection cut out at the time you are all supposed to share your clay sculpture of how your womb will look at nine months.

In my area, there were a multitude of options. I chose a general class held at the hospital at which we were planning to have the baby. This was fortunate, because we also got a tour of the hospital that showed us important sites like the birthing rooms and where a vending machine that sold only Hot Pockets was located. I also got some tips that ended up being helpful during the actual birth—the instructor had given birth both with an epidural and without one, and she talked about the pros and cons to both options. She also covered some different labor and birth positions and breathing exercises that I did end up using. I also felt like the class gave me a more thorough explanation of what to expect during labor and birth, which helped me to plan for it a little better. At the class I attended, I even chatted with some like-minded parents-to-be, who I never saw again—but I do have friends who forged close ties with some people they met at birth classes, so that could happen to you.

After successfully completing any baby prep classes, you will probably need to down a couple of mocktails.

Mocktails for the Parent-to-Be

I Just Survived a Phone Call-Rita: After you accomplish making an actual phone call, place lemonade and ice into a blender. Pour the blended mixture into a margarita glass, close your eyes, and imagine you are on a remote island where people can only communicate via text message.

Reason to be Excused Tea: When at a party where you don't know anyone, slam several glasses of iced tea and then excuse yourself to go to the bathroom. Use the one back at your own house.

Online Forum Agua Fresca: Read a post in your online pregnancy forum about someone having a pregnancy complication. After googling said complication for a couple of hours and calculating the odds of you getting it too, take a break to go to a Mexican restaurant and order several rounds of agua frescas and queso.

Hydration Flask: It's important for pregnant people to stay hydrated. Fill a flask with tap water and keep it in your pocket. Every time someone touches your belly without asking permission, pull it out and take a drink.

Pregnancy Shots: Just fill a shot glass with your favorite flavor of LaCroix, and take a drink every time:

- Someone asks if you are happy or disappointed it's a boy or a girl.
- Someone asks if you've seen *The Business of Being Born*.
- Someone asks what you plan to do with the placenta.
- Someone asks if you should be eating whatever thing you are eating.
- You go to bed at the end of every day and when you wake up every morning.

3

Expecting Another Way

If you are becoming a parent via adoption, surrogacy, or some sort of *Baby Boom*–type inheritance, then you will be managing plenty of awkward social situations as you prepare for your child's arrival. You will need to attend classes, prepare for parenthood, and negotiate questions from family and friends. You may also be navigating a lot of red tape, additional phone calls, and meetings as you prepare to bring your child home.

FINDING YOUR SMALL VILLAGE

Connecting with a few other parents-to-be who understand where you are coming from can be helpful. So, as much as you might prefer to stay home in your pajamas, signing up for some classes or other expecting-parent groups can help you navigate the new experiences. If you get halfway into the first meeting and realize you have made the wrong choice, you can always just pretend to get a very important phone call and bolt. Or you can find an online discussion board or Facebook group that allows you to connect with people while you're still in your pajamas. Just look for one that has like-minded people and spends at least 50 percent of the time discussing useful information rather than devolving into arguments in all-caps.

MANAGING INVASIVE QUESTIONS

If you are becoming a parent in a nontraditional way, then friends or family members may have questions—maybe a lot of questions. Once your child arrives, random strangers might also make assumptions about your situation. A parent with an adopted child might get mistaken for the nanny. A friend of mine who *was* a nanny said that people always assumed the child she was watching was her son, despite the fact that her age and the child's age meant that it was very unlikely that she was his mother. People on the street are confused! Unfortunately, there is no class called "Conversations with strangers on the street: Dos and don'ts," so you will have to do some on-the-fly explaining.

A Few Questions You May Hear

- Why didn't you try [insert laughable or obvious thing]?
- I bet you'll get pregnant now.

- Is that your real child?
- Where did you get her from?
- Whose egg or sperm did you use?
- How much did it cost?

SOME WAYS TO RESPOND TO INVASIVE QUESTIONS

Embrace your facial expressions: When you are on the quieter side, people sometimes assume that you are not that approachable. You've probably spent a good chunk of your life being told that you should become more approachable. But good news! You can ignore that advice and now strategically use your resting introvert face to get people to leave you alone.

Develop stock answers: Once you've heard the same question several times you can assume that you will hear it again, so coming up with a response that you are comfortable using will help. Or just print out and laminate a "FAQs About My Child" card to hand out to people on the street.

Pretend to mishear people: Some questions from friends or acquaintances will inevitably crop up. So you can always just act like you didn't hear the question right: "How much does adopting a squid cost? I'm not sure. You should probably ask at the aquarium."

SELF-CARE TIPS

Managing a lot of different people's questions and expectations can be exhausting. Take some time to create some self-care:

1. **Don't feel bad about saying no.** Feel free to turn down 100 percent of invitations to dinner parties, work networking events, and information-gathering sessions disguised as coffee meetups.
2. **Eat right to feel good.** Pie for breakfast can be a real mood lifter.
3. **Get outside.** Maybe take a walk around the block or to your favorite restaurant to buy pie.
4. **Read a book.** Luckily, you are one step ahead of the game because you're already reading one!
5. **Light a candle.** Or a full-on bonfire. Go ahead and burn whatever you want to in the flames.
6. **At the end of the day, write down three good things about your day.** After listing your three things, feel free to write a diary entry rant about something you can't believe someone asked you. It's never too early to start gathering material for your tell-all book.

4

Sharing the News

When I was pregnant, I jokingly told an acquaintance that I kind of wished I could just keep the entire pregnancy a secret and then show up one day with a baby. She then told me that she had actually done that with her now-grown child. She was living abroad at the time and didn't want her mother to worry about her, so she kept her pregnancy a secret until she one day returned home to visit with a baby. So if you happen to be living abroad in a time before social media and video calls, then I highly recommend this method. As for everyone else, you will probably need to find a way to share the news before the baby arrives. If you are becoming a parent after fertility treatments or through adoption, you will also need to decide how many details you want to share with others. Telling people the news can trigger a lot of questions and expectations, so like most everything else in your life, it can take some consideration.

Sharing the news that you are expecting a child, or now have a child, has become its own industry. People will create elaborate announcements, videos, and parties to spread the news. In the age of social media, many people spend time orchestrating complicated announcements to broadcast across all their channels. If that is your thing—go for it. But if the thought of booking a professional photographer to take a picture of you wearing an embroidered hat that says "Soon we will be three" ranks right up there with playing charades with strangers, then you will need to find a different way to tell people.

COMMUNICATION METHOD POSSIBILITIES

There are lots of methods to choose from—but there are some pros and cons to each of them.

- **Face-to-face**: Some people who you are telling may prefer or appreciate this method, but proceed with caution, because it involves a lot of eye contact.
- **Over the phone**: This is a decent option for someone you want to tell more personally or who you know will ask a lot of questions that you are willing to answer, but it's not super-efficient. So think about the number of phone calls you are willing to make before proceeding.
- **In writing**: This is probably your preferred method of communication because you can think through what you will say. Feel free to handwrite, type, or cross-stitch your news.
- **Gossipy person**: In this helpful method, you tell one person who can't keep a secret and then wait 24 hours.

By then everyone else will know, and you will have only had to convey the news once. If I have something I need to tell people but I'm feeling anxious about it for whatever reason, I sometimes tell a friend or family member and ask them to tell other people. Some people would probably call this a cop-out, but I call it an effective communication strategy.

ANNOUNCEMENT OPTIONS

There is no rule saying you must formally announce anything. Tell people you feel like telling and the rest will find out eventually. When I was pregnant, I just told people as a I felt like it—starting with close family members and then moving on to friends and others from there. Most people found out. Some acquaintances from high school still don't know. But once you decide you're going to go public, and have selected a communication method, you'll have to decide on the specifics of the actual announcement:

- **Email**: You can always send a digital card out to friends and family members that includes the news, and do something fun like add an image of six babies to keep them guessing.
- **Card**: The beauty of a printed card is that it's hard for people to hit reply and start asking you whether you are planning to get an epidural.
- **Group text**: Already on an endless group chat discussing when you will meet up with friends for a dinner? Just send a quick mass text: "I'm pregnant and I'm not

going to send you a selfie and you are not invited to the birth." Simple. Easy.

- **Anonymous announcement:** Drawing on inspiration from ransom-note Pinterest boards, cut out letters from magazines to spell out the words: "Someone you know is becoming a parent" and then glue them to a blank piece of paper. Put the paper in an envelope without including a return address and mail it. Clever recipients will be able to guess the identity of the future parent based on the postmark.

WHAT YOU CAN LEARN FROM CELEBRITIES WHO SUCCESSFULLY HID THEIR PARENTING STATUS FOR MONTHS

If you decide to put off revealing the news for a while, or select the "surprise baby" announcement option, you can take a page from a celebrity's book for ways to hide your parenthood news for a while.

- **Celebrity:** Actors Eva Mendes and Ryan Gosling kept their second baby a secret until after she was born in 2016.[*] Mendes was photographed in public later in her pregnancy, but she still managed to keep the news under wraps.
  Takeaway: Holding a bag in front of your belly when you go out in public is a good way to obscure a baby bump.

---

* elite daily, "Ryan Gosling and Eva Mendes Had a Secret Baby Nobody Knew About," www.elitedaily.com/entertainment/eva -mendes-ryan-gosling-had-baby/1488858.

- **Celebrity**: Since giving birth to her daughter in 2017, Mindy Kaling has managed to keep the identity of the child's father under wraps. When she gave birth to a son in 2020, she also kept the father's identity (and her pregnancy) a secret.[*]

  Takeaway: You do not need to reveal who the father of your child is to friends or major news outlets.

- **Celebrity**: Actress Rachel McAdams didn't confirm that she had become a mother until her son was seven months old.[†]

  Takeaway: If you starred in the movie *The Notebook,* you are very good at keeping your baby news under wraps.

- **Celebrity**: In January of 2020, Cameron Diaz announced the birth of her daughter but kept the details surrounding the birth private, leading some to speculate whether she became a parent via surrogacy or adoption.[‡]

  Takeaway: There is no need to explain how you became a parent.

---

[*] Showbiz CheatSheet, "Who Is the Father of Mindy Kaling's Children? Kaling Has a Specific Reason for Staying Mum," www.cheatsheet.com/entertainment/who-is-the-father-of-mindy-kalings-kids.html.

[†] *People,* "How Rachel McAdams Kept Her Pregnancy a Secret Before Welcoming Baby Boy," https://people.com/movies/how-rachel-mcadams-kept-her-pregnancy-a-secret-before-welcoming-baby-boy.

[‡] Insider, "Cameron Diaz Had a Baby at 47, and She Doesn't Owe Us an Explanation of How She Did It," www.insider.com/cameron-diaz-baby-47-fans-want-to-know-how-2020-1.

- **Celebrity**: Actress Rashida Jones and musician Ezra Koenig never revealed that they were dating or expecting a child.*

Takeaway: If you are single, one option for avoiding questions at the next family gathering about whether you are dating anyone is to just show up with a baby.

---

* *People,* "26 Celebs Who Were Really, Really Good at Keeping Their Baby News a Secret," https://people.com/parents/celebrities -who-hid-their-pregnancies/?slide=5593356#5593356.

5

Panic! at the Baby Shower

Before I was pregnant, going to baby showers was usually socially exhausting for me. It often involved making small talk with people I didn't know, and I didn't love most baby shower games. But as an attendee, I was always kind of relieved that I got to hang back in the corner during the gift-opening event and could spend time sipping a mimosa and catching up with friends I hadn't seen in a while.

But being the guest of honor at a traditional baby shower is the adult introvert's version of showing up to junior high naked. If you are the one gestating the baby, you are supposed to drink champagne-free orange juice (unless it's unpasteurized, then you should just have water) while opening millions of newborn-sized onesies while everyone stares at you. As a bonus, you may also be pressured to give up your list of baby names so that someone can tell you their second cousin once heard of someone having a bully at school with that same name. Celebrating the upcoming arrival of a child and showering the parent-to-be with gifts and advice is a lovely idea, but some of the elements of the traditional baby shower can be intimidating if you don't love being the center of attention. For overthinkers, showers can also churn up social stresses about whether different friends and family members are going to get along, how your friends who are having difficulty conceiving will feel attending, and whether someone is going to make you wear a crown made of diapers.

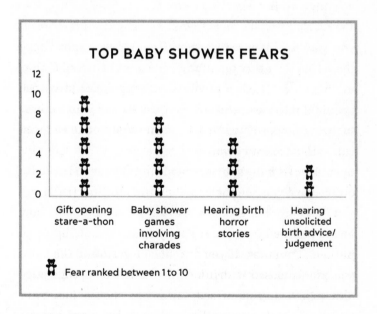

THE SETUP

You may not get to choose what kind of shower you have, because some people have their own visions when it comes to baby showers, and you are probably trying to avoid turning into an ExpectingParentZilla by micro-managing the details of the party. But if you are asked to weigh in, then there are some options:

Say no: There is no rule that says you must have a baby shower if you don't want one. People will call you a spoil-sport and a loser and probably throw a surprise party for you anyway. But hey, it's worth a try.

The couple party: It's ideal to take some of the attention off yourself, so if you have a significant other, you can rope them into the event too. If the person is extroverted, they might enjoy it. If they are introverted, you can share the spotlight together, reluctantly. A couple party also seems to throw people off track since it isn't traditional, and that can make it less awkward.

Guest lists: At baby showers, some people like to invite lit-erally everyone and their mother. But if big parties stress you out, a smaller group is better. So if you can somehow have a party with just one or two people, then do that. Peo-ple with large families or groups of friends might also consider breaking things up into more than one shower—although you will have to weigh whether one big shower or a couple of smaller ones would cause you more stress.

Lobby for different gift opening: Parts of a baby shower aren't so bad—binge-eating tiny sandwiches and catching up with friends you haven't seen in a while can be, as Martha Stewart would say, a good thing. But one of the big problems is the spotlight gift opening event in which everyone stares at a guest of honor while they open presents. So, see if you can do something different—like having a special intimate gift opening room where you go with each member of the party one at a time to chat and open the gift. Or do something completely unorthodox, like not open the gifts at the party.

Have a diaper shower: A diaper shower is another way to circumvent the gift opening event, particularly if you already have a lot of hand-me-downs and are pretty set in the baby items department. You will need a lot of diapers—more diapers than you will even want to think about. Even if you are planning to use cloth diapers, you will need a stockpile to use when the thought of doing another load of laundry makes you retreat to the couch to cry. The diaper shower can take some of the focus off you because people are probably less invested in watching you open a jumbo box of really amazing leakproof diapers than a cute baby tiara.

Make it casual: Traditional showers sometimes involve people getting dressed up and sipping tea with one pinky in the air. But if being dressed casually and keeping your pinky attached to a cup is more comfortable for you, then request to keep things more casual.

Choose a really distracting setting: If you are worried about how your devout great aunt is going to make small talk with your atheist roommate from college, then it may be better to have the event in a distracting setting. Think about loud places where there are a lot of obstructed views—perhaps a casino or Chuck E Cheese (you might as well start getting used to it now).

VIRTUAL BABY SHOWERS

Sometimes an in-person baby shower isn't possible because the expecting parent is on bedrest, lives far from family and friends, or is living through a global pandemic. If you were not that excited about a traditional shower, you may have just won the get-out-of-the-baby-shower free card. Congrats!

But others may still insist you have a shower. If so, you may find that a virtual shower is an appealing option since you can attend while wearing sweatpants. But a lot of the same rules for in-person baby showers apply to virtual showers in that you should try to make the event fit what you will be comfortable with. When I was expecting, someone on a baby message board said her relatives wanted to have a virtual shower in which they all drank a bunch of wine and then watched her open presents via video. This idea kind of horrified her, and honestly the idea of that horrified me too. If having a long video call devoted to you performing gift opening for an audience feels like some sort of reality show gone wrong, then opt out of the gift opening portion of the program. Keeping the shower short and using it as a way to catch up with people you haven't seen in a while is a good option. If someone really wants to see you open their gift, you can always set up a separate one-on-one chat with them. Some virtual shower guidelines also suggest flipping the gift opening on the participants—have each of them open the gift they got you (that they can send to you later) and then maybe they can talk about how they found it useful and/or why a baby can never have too many tutus.

BABY SHOWER GAMES FOR PEOPLE WHO DON'T LIKE BABY SHOWER GAMES

Some people like baby shower games. You are probably not one of those people. Common staples include making guests eat baby food or inspect melted chocolate in diapers. Other activities include bobbing for baby bottle nipples or doing some elaborate game that makes participants simulate peeing like a pregnant woman. A lot of these games involve teaming up with people you don't know to do one of these tasks, so it's like spending your Saturday at a team-building retreat at a new job. The type of baby shower games that I don't mind are ones that allow me to stay seated and are more like a trivia night than an improv show—guess the celebrity baby name, guess the price of a baby product, and so forth. So those were the types of games I requested at my baby shower. If you aren't able to sell your host on not having games at all, then here are some alternative ideas.

- **Chocolate feast:** A traditional game involves melting various kinds of chocolate bars in a diaper and having guests try to guess what kind of chocolate bar it was. If this does not sound fun to you, then try this new spin on the game—basically, you just put out some chocolate bars on the table and everyone eats them.

- **Introvert versus extroverts**: Divide up the guests based on who likes playing games versus who doesn't like to. Then let the extroverts play games while the introverts talk quietly or just sit in the corners eating cute tiny finger foods.
- **Top five favorite books**: Everyone writes a list of their top favorite books of all time and some brief notes about why they like them. Then they hand them to the parent-to-be to take home and review at a later time, when no one is watching. This doesn't have anything to do with babies, which is why it is a good game.
- **Axe throwing**: This activity has become popular and is probably a good way to work out your stress and anxiety. Since some people also like to decorate stuff at baby showers, you can first have guests bedazzle their axes.

AFTER THE PARTY

Congrats! You survived the party and probably now have a diaper genie and enough newborn-sized outfits so that your child can wear a new outfit every hour of the day for the zero to three weeks they fit into that size of clothing. Do something to reward yourself for getting through one of the first big introverted parenting obstacles, like slamming a pitcher of virgin mojitos or lying alone in a dark room for an hour or two.

6

If You Overthink Things and You Know It: Selecting a Baby Name

Some people have baby names that appear to them in a dream while they're in junior high school and then they spend several years practicing writing the names in cursive pastel letters in various notebooks. When these people become parents, their chosen names are magically the very ones that their partner and friends and family also love and thus the process of naming their children is easy and stress-free. If this sounds like your story, you should contact the publishers of Ripley's Believe It or Not! and skip this chapter. If your experience is different than this, read on. This chapter is for the people who approach baby naming like a jury deliberation in an espionage trial. If your tendency is to think things through before making a decision or if you are hyperaware of what other people think, deciding what to name your child can be a big task.

When my husband and I were trying to decide on a name for our first child, I felt the need to consider almost every name possible. (This is not surprising, considering that I am also the type of person who needs to consider every item on several virtual menus before ordering takeout.) Selecting a kid's name felt like a big responsibility because there are a lot of considerations when it comes to names and it is something the person would have for life—or at least until they are old enough to go online and fill out a legally binding name change form. While pregnant, any name I encountered became a possible name. I spent too much time on baby name message boards and considered names in books I was reading and TV shows I was watching or had ever watched. I briefly lobbied for the name of a character on the TV show *Felicity*, until my husband vetoed it. My husband is into cycling, so I spent part of the summer I was pregnant considering names of the riders, announcers, and various random objects in the televised coverage of the Tour de France. By the time of my son's birth, we had narrowed it down to a short list of names and then made the final decision when he was born. So if you are reading this well in advance of having a child on the way, you better start thinking about names now.

A PARTIAL LIST OF THINGS YOU WILL DELIBERATE WHEN DECIDING ON A BABY NAME

Initials: People say you should check the initials of a name to make sure they don't spell out something like SOS or ASS. And to confuse things further, monograms sometimes list the letters as first name, last name, middle name, so you have to consider whether little Rowan Taylor Anderson will one day be gifted a towel with the letters RAT printed on it.

Too common: People who grew up with five other people with the same name in their class or workplace often want a less common name for their baby, so that in the future they don't keep getting confused with that other Ashley at work—the one who keeps talking about synergy.

Too unusual: On the other hand, people are concerned about names that are too unusual. What if the kid has to repeat their name a lot? How will they cope with never being able to find a novelty keychain with their name on it?

Spelling: Once you decide on a name that you like, you can then begin overthinking how to spell it. If there are different common spellings, which do you choose? Do you use a slightly different spelling to make it unusual while accepting the fact that it will forever be incorrectly spelled on Starbucks cups?

Pronunciation: Sometimes a name can be pronounced different ways, but parents want it to be pronounced only a certain way. No matter how hard you try, some percentage of people will still end up pronouncing Andrea as Hydrangea.

Rhyming: Some people think rhyming names are fun. Some people think rhyming names are awful. Some people just give up and use an unpronounceable symbol as a name.

Pet names: When I was lurking on baby name message boards, some posters would say that certain names sound too much like dog names so they shouldn't be used for children. So, you know what would help? If people just start calling all dogs Mr. WoofyPants.

Previous bad associations: If you, your significant other, or any friends or family members had a school bully with a name you are considering, then it may need to get nixed. Making decisions like this are particularly hard if you work in a profession where you encounter a lot of different names, like teaching or moderating an online parenting discussion group.

Can you shout the name?: Someone told me to try shouting the name to make sure it's easy to get out. You know, in case you ever need to call your child to come in for dinner and not for those days when you reach the end of your rope.

Nicknames: Some people are big on nicknames from the start—"We've named her Vivienne but we are going to call her Maude," or, "His first name is Istanbul but we will be calling him by his middle name, Constantinople." Other people are big on choosing names that can't be turned into nicknames, because it could cause confusion down the line when the time comes for them to put their name on a personalized gold chain necklace.

Family names or initials: Sometimes people have a certain letter they want to work with, or they want to work a family name into the first or middle name. But if they choose one family member or one side of the family, will the other side get mad? There is only one way to find out.

Associations with famous bad people: Is the name shared by an obscure king who started wars or rolled around on piles of gold and drank dissolved pearls? Sometimes it's good to check.

Name meanings: When I was searching for baby names, I sometimes made the mistake of looking up name meanings. I discovered that, like many other parenting topics, the meanings of the names were often conflicting. One site would say the name meant, "loyal and trustworthy" while another would indicate it meant, "one who steals chickens."

Whether a celebrity has the name: Depending on your thoughts on this, you might either go searching for celebrity names, or you might create a list of names to avoid because it is a celebrity name.

"Type" of name: People have a lot of ideas about the type of person that a name evokes, and they will say certain names indicate something like "girl next door" or "mean girl." However, if your child turns into an undesirable stereotype, then you probably can't blame it on the name.

Middle names: When I entered the fray of baby name message boards, I would inevitably encounter people who were extremely focused on what the first name sounded like with the middle name: "What do you think sounds more regal—Michael Henry or Michael Alexander?" Of course, in 20 years approximately only 1 percent of Michael's friends will even know what his middle name is, but still, it can be extremely important when discussing names on the internet with strangers.

Siblings: If you already have a child or are having more than one child, then you have to also consider how the sibling names sound with each other and how quickly you can yell multiple names at once.

What the child looks like: Some people say that you can't really name a child until you see them. Once they are born, you can look at them to tell what kind of name best suits them. If you are using this approach, you can plan ahead by bringing a binder of pictures of famous bald people to the delivery room.

OTHER CONSIDERATIONS

Sharing the names: Given that baby names inspire a lot of opinions, one of the biggest decisions is whether to share or announce your baby names with others. A lot of people recommend not announcing the name until after the baby is born, since doing that means there will potentially be less debate. Some people even look for the most unique name in the history of names and guard their chosen name like it's the location of the Batcave.

Weighing others' opinions: If you don't have a significant other, then you can ultimately make your own decision.

Your friends and other family members may have opinions too, but they don't really get voting rights. If you do have a spouse or partner, then you'll need to get them to agree to a name or begin plotting a secret Major Major Major birth certificate naming deception.

FAQ: Selecting a Baby Name

Q I've tried reading through the baby name chapter and still can't decide on a name. What should I do?

A Close your eyes and point to a name in a baby name book.

Q I hate the name that I pointed to.

A Look, no one said that it was going to be a good name. It was just an idea.

Q Can I do it again?

A Sure. But don't complain if it still isn't right.

PLACES TO GO FISHING FOR BABY NAMES

- **Books:** Some people search for biblical or literary names, or they just start thumbing through an architectural design coffee table book out of desperation.
- **TV:** You, too, can go fishing for names by watching the Tour de France or whatever TV shows you are into—perhaps a cooking show or C-SPAN?
- **Family trees:** Even if none of the names work out, you should at least be entertained.

- **Online baby name lists:** You could make a full-time job out of reading all the books and online lists of baby names. Unfortunately, it's an unpaid job.
- **The natural world:** Take a walk and consider flower, tree, or particularly interesting rock names.
- **Collect names:** Solicit opinions from friends and family members and collect baby name ideas from them. If you end up using a name that someone suggests, you can buy that person a box of chocolates or a ham.
- **The produce aisle:** If it works for Gwyneth Paltrow, maybe it will work for you?*

---

* *Today's Parent*, "Gwyneth Paltrow explains the name 'Apple'!," www.todaysparent.com/uncategorized/gwyneth-paltrow-explains -the-name-apple.

PART TWO

SURVIVING THE
FIRST YEAR

7

Showtime: The Birth

During the birth class I attended, we watched a video of a couple talking about the day of their birth. When the woman went into labor, the couple spent a lot of time at home before heading to the hospital. They went on walks and she took a bath and rested. At one point, the husband said something like, "It was a really relaxing day." I was pretty sure parts of that day were not all that relaxing, particularly for the woman, but I did like the idea of trying to stay home for the early stages of labor before heading to the hospital. Not because the 1980s birth couple painted such a rosy picture, but because I knew labor could take a long time and it didn't seem like I needed to be in a hurry to get to the hospital. I had some anxiety about the fact that the baby was going to eventually need to come out of my body, so having a basic plan for how the day might look helped me feel better.

The day before my son's due date was my birthday, so I was working from home and getting ready to drive to meet my husband for lunch when I felt a little bit of liquid leak. It was not the huge rush of water that I imagined your water breaking would be, so at first, I thought about just going to the lunch. But instead, I called my doctor's office and described what was going on, and they said it sounded like my water had broken and I needed to get to the hospital right away. No time to lounge around and have a "relaxing" day at home! Despite my desire to plan things, I realized that some of my plans had gone out the window.

Although not everything will probably go according to plan, it will still help to do some planning. And there are some social aspects of the birth for you to consider before the baby or babies you have been gestating need to come out.

WHO TO HAVE IN THE ROOM DURING LABOR

Who wouldn't want to be naked from *at least* the waist down in a room full of 3 to 20 people? Most normal people. But, when it comes to having a baby, this is a plausible scenario. Some people seem to invite roughly everyone on their holiday card mailing list to watch the birth of a child, but chances are that will probably not work for you.

Depending on your friends or family members, navigating the "who will be in the room" question can be tricky and personal. Even so, your job is to decide on both a birth location and the people who will be there that will make you most comfortable.

One thing I didn't expect was how much time I would spend with the labor and delivery nurses during the course of giving birth and during the couple of days in the hospital afterward. A series of different nurses rotated through during our stay, and they often had different styles. The nurse who helped me through my first son's birth was a good mix of comforting and reassuring (although she did also congratulate me on my advanced maternal age, since I had checked into the hospital on the day I turned 35, but I let that go). It felt natural to have her in the room throughout the labor and delivery, which was fortunate, since it was kind of her job to be there the whole time.

I kept the number of visitors small when I went into labor—a few family members were in the hospital but not in the actual room once my son was on his way out. During the final stages of labor, it was just me, my husband, a doctor, and a nurse, and that felt like the right number for me. I have friends who, during their birthing process, wanted a supportive friend, relative, or doula in the room as well, but I just wanted to keep it small.

If you have a relative or friend who is insisting on being there when you don't want them to be, you've got a couple of options:

- **Say no:** It's your birth and you can avoid certain people if you want to.
- **Use your nurse/doula/aggressive friend as a bouncer:** If you aren't up for a confrontation, chances are you know people who will do a good job at protecting your space. A lot of people will like being assigned some sort of task that they can help you with. Use them.
- **Stall:** It's probably up to you to call your friends and relatives when you go into labor and you can put off doing that as long as you want—hours, days even.
- **Explain that visitors aren't allowed at the hospital/ birthing center/your home birth:** Sorry. But rules are rules.

If you are not the one who will actually be having the baby come out of your body, then not being in the birth spotlight might be a bit of a relief. You can spend your time lending assistance whenever possible. If the person in labor doesn't mind a lot of people and attention, then you, as the assistant, may get to take some short breaks from time to time to hide in the bathroom. If the person giving birth doesn't love the attention, then you can help play defense by keeping visitors to a minimum. Meanwhile, do what you can to share the pain.

THE BIRTH PLAN

Any expecting parent who has entered the arena of the birth discussion forums knows that the minutiae of pregnancy and The Birth are discussed endlessly. A lot of thought is given to the birth plan—basically a written outline of how you would like things to go. What do you want to wear? Who will be in the room? Do you want drugs and, if so, what kind? Do you require a very specific flavor of Popsicle? Of course, as I found out, you can plan all you want but things might change. Still, you'll probably want to have some sort of plan.

Birth Plan Template

(Select all that apply):

🍼 **Please note that I am:**

____ Introverted

____ Socially anxious

____ Just kind of tired of people right now

🍼 **People allowed in the room:**

____ My partner

____ My doula

____ George Clooney, if dressed like his *ER* character Doug Ross

🍼 **People not allowed in the room:**

____ Everyone else

🍼 **Topics that aren't allowed:**

____ The weather

____ Birth horror stories

____ Commentaries on a parent's age

Birth Plan Template *(continued)*

(Select all that apply):

🍼 **The room environment should include:**

____ Soft music

____ Calming voices

____ Lighting so dark it's kind of hard to see people and body parts

🍼 **I'd like to spend the first stage of labor:**

____ On a birth ball

____ Walking around

____ Lying in bed binge-watching *Schitt's Creek*

🍼 **I'd like friends and family members to:**

____ Briefly join me after the birth

____ Visit in groups no larger than two people

____ Silently hand me a plate of sushi and bottle of whiskey as a congratulatory gift and then slowly back out of the room

🍼 **I'd like to designate the following person to make small talk for me:**

____ My partner

____ My doula

____ My extroverted friend Chloe

AFTER BABY ARRIVES

After the baby arrives, you will probably be spending a lot of time trying to figure out how to feed them and change diapers and do minor things like get some sleep. When I had my first son, there was a steady stream of visitors coming through my hospital room—doctors, nurses, lactation consultants, and friends and family members. Since a lot of those people were providing much needed advice and support, I wasn't overwhelmed with all the visits. But holding off on visits from friends and family until you get home and are more settled is an option. Since I was trying to learn how to breastfeed (which was about 1,000 times more difficult than the breastfeeding class and books had made it seem), I was keeping our son in the room with us.

On our second night in the hospital, the night nurse asked me and my husband if we wanted her to take our son to the nursery so we could get some sleep. I was hesitant to do it—a lot of breastfeeding advice made it sound like if you separated from your baby for more than an hour your milk supply would dry up and your kid would never score above 900 on their SATs. But I was also exhausted. I kind of half-heartedly said no and then she basically told us it was a good idea to get some rest, and we could come get him whenever we wanted, so we said sure. She took him to the nursery, and I got the first several hours of solid sleep in a row that I would get for a while after we arrived back home. I still think of letting that nurse take the baby to the nursery as one of the best early decisions we made.

If your baby did not arrive in a way that you expected, you may be tempted to start overthinking how things should or could have gone differently. But you are probably also exhausted and learning how to take care of a small human, so try to give yourself a break. Now that you are parent, there are plenty more opportunities for overthinking to come.

8

Social Overload: Managing Well-Meaning Friends and Family

 When I was pregnant with my first child, I quickly realized that the birth industrial complex means that a lot of people put a ton of planning into having the baby but significantly less planning into what happens after the baby arrives. I was anxious about the pregnancy and birth part, but because I like to think ahead, I also tried to do some planning for the post-birth part. This turned out to be helpful, because after having the child I had a bunch of meals in the freezer and a list of lactation consultants I could call when I was at the end of my rope with breastfeeding (which occurred roughly on day three). Still, I could have planned a bit better. A bunch of people kept asking me if I was going to have a birth doula or whether or not I would get an epidural, but no one asked me if I had a year's supply of dry shampoo or if I thought about hiring a postpartum doula (which, spoiler alert, I think would have been really helpful for me to have).

One thing I didn't take into account is how much socializing can happen immediately after you become a parent. Once you have a child, a lot of people will be interested in meeting the little one and you'll have to decide if you want them to come for a visit and how long you want them to stay. (Just be glad you aren't a member of a royal family, like Kate Middleton, who had a good portion of the world interested in meeting her babies and so she had to pose for a family photo session on the day she gave birth to each child.)

When we got home from the hospital, we initially had a lot of visitors. But when we went to our first pediatrician appointment a few days later, my son's birth weight wasn't where they wanted it to be. So my pediatrician told me to stop having visitors for a while to give me time to focus on figuring out breastfeeding. Getting permission to take a pause on visitors was kind of a relief.

Some visitors will be slightly more helpful than others, so you may need to create a social triage system, as explained below.

EVALUATION CRITERIA FOR VISITORS

- **How are they helping?** Are they going to hold the baby while you nap or do they happen to be a gourmet chef?
- **How long do they tend to stay?** Were they always the

last person to leave a party or do they know how to keep a visit brief?

- **How much do they stress you out?** If having someone visit or stay with you under normal circumstances is tough, then it will likely be worse during the new baby period since you will be undergoing your own personal sleep deprivation torture study.

- **What is their experience with babies?** Have they recently had a baby and can offer you some help/guidance? Are they a baby whisperer? Is it Dr. Harvey Karp, author of *The Happiest Baby on the Block*? If so, consider admitting them.

HOW TO SCARE OFF UNWANTED VISITORS FROM EVER COMING AGAIN

Many visitors will get the hint that you need some space, but others may need a little more encouragement. Here are some ways to scare off the latter:

- **Figure out what your child's witching hour is and invite the visitor over then.** Not even Harvey Karp can handle a kid screaming at the top of their lungs for an hour on end without wanting to get away from the noise.

- **Go out for a little bit and leave them alone to babysit.** The more babies you have, the better.

- **Make overnight visitors take a shift getting up with the baby.** Who says quality time with the baby needs to be during daylight hours?

- **Get a dog that barks at all new people.** Barking + crying baby = alone time.
- **Blast "Baby Shark" on a loop all day.** No one will ever be able to stay for long.

PARENTING AMNESIA

When you are trying to figure out how to raise a small human, you will inevitably go looking for some sort of advice. When I became a parent, one of the more overwhelming things was confronting the sheer amount of conflicting advice I found about what I should be doing. Since I'm prone to information gathering, I read a lot of different advice. I was surprised at how often even the experts directly contradicted each other on different topics. For example, depending on who I listened to, the answer to getting my baby to sleep was: 1) doing nothing, 2) doing a serious and complex intervention, or 3) buying a magical essential oil from a remote region of the Himalayas.

Among these experts are other parents. When getting advice from other parents, there is a phenomenon that you will quickly become familiar with: parenting amnesia. People who are parents have a lot of advice, and sometimes that advice is helpful and other times that advice is something like, "I don't remember my babies *ever* crying." Some people like to keep things positive, but when you are dealing with a new, stressed-out parent, the last thing they want to hear about is how amazing their friend's baby is or was at doing the thing that their baby is not doing. What's more, if the advice-givers are parents, they have probably endured years of sleep deprivation, which has made their memories spotty, at best. Or they raised kids during an era when babies rode home from the hospital in a box in the back of a pickup truck, and therefore they have slightly different ideas about what is safe.

Parenting guidelines also change quickly, and all kids are different. The parent of one well-behaved child may think they've got everything figured out, but by the second or third child they realize they were just lucky the first time around. After having a kid, I also realized that my memory of what exactly had happened got spotty quickly. A friend would ask what a certain baby stage a few months prior had been like and I couldn't quite remember all the details. People's ability to remember the details of how their baby behaved several years earlier is highly suspect.

If you are talking to someone who has parenting amnesia, then you can just smile and nod and take the advice that seems helpful and disregard the stuff that seems like it came from the Betty Draper handbook of child rearing.

Signs the Person You Are Talking to Has Parenting Amnesia:

- They say that their baby never cried, never had trouble sleeping, or never had a diaper blow out.
- They start sentences with the words, "Back in my day ..."
- They look into the eyes of a parent of a colicky baby who hasn't slept for more than one hour at a time for

several weeks and say, "You'll miss these days when they're over."

- They say, "Well, I always filled my baby's bottle with whiskey to help her sleep, and she turned out just fine."

Speaking of feeding your baby whiskey, let's move along to the complicated area of feeding your baby.

9

Nourishment with a Dash of Judgement: Feeding Your Baby

Perhaps no other baby subject has racked up more social media diatribes and online fights than the feeding of babies. The basic options are breastfeeding, formula feeding, or a combination of both. Choices about which to do include complicated questions about health, money, resources, work, and how many children you have. People tend to have strong opinions about their methods, which means that you will probably have to expel some mental energy discussing your choice. And if you live in your own head a lot, you may spend a lot of time ruminating over the various details and opinions about how to feed your baby.

I decided to try breastfeeding my first child, and from talking to friends, I knew that breastfeeding wasn't always easy. But I didn't appreciate just how tough it could be until I was holding a three-day-old baby who, when I tried to feed him, started screaming and writhing and acting like I was trying to get him to suck on a lemon. For me, it took a lot of time to breastfeed my newborn—sometimes as long as 45 minutes, and sometimes the baby needed to eat as soon as an hour and a half after I had first begun my previous session. So the math didn't really add up to me being able to do much else. Advice in this arena was also confusing and contradictory. Some people said breastfeeding shouldn't hurt, but a lactation consultant at the hospital told me that it was going to hurt some. A lot of breastfeeding books told me that I shouldn't let the baby have a bottle for a few weeks or they would refuse the breast. But a lot of moms reported that if you didn't introduce them to a bottle sooner, then the baby would refuse to take a bottle. Since I needed to return to work and was interested in occasionally being able to leave the house without a small human attached to me, I wanted my baby to be able to take a bottle as well as breastfeed.

An added layer of stress and confusion for me was that my son wasn't initially gaining weight quickly, something that some people said was probably not a big deal and would work itself out and others said was a big deal to be concerned about. When I was breastfeeding, it was hard for me to tell when my son had gotten enough milk—people make it seem like this will be a natural thing that you will just *know*, but I found it hard to tell since he wasn't yet talking. Some people would say they could tell if their baby was hungry because of a specific kind of cry, but all the cries sounded pretty much the same to me. So I breastfed and then supplemented with some formula to help him gain weight. After weeks of lactation consultant visits and breastfeeding classes where I could gather with other sleep-deprived women to weigh our babies before and after a feeding, I made peace with the fact that it would be okay to just switch to formula (and if you are making this choice, I highly recommend Hanna Rosin's *Atlantic* article on the subject).* Things got a bit easier, so I continued breastfeeding and sometimes supplementing with formula for about six months when I had to stop breastfeeding completely for medical reasons. And I can report that my child has not (yet) turned to a life of crime. I have friends who exclusively breastfed for longer and others who chose formula from the start, and in all cases their children also appear to be functioning just fine. So, at the end of the day, trust that a variety of different options will work.

"FUN" QUESTIONS AND COMMENTS ABOUT HOW YOU ARE FEEDING YOUR BABY

When You Choose to Breastfeed

- Didn't you just feed the baby?
- Shouldn't you be feeding the baby?
- Are you sure the baby got enough milk? Do you know they need to get the rich hindmilk? What about the extremely rich platinum milk?
- Have you tried the football hold/cross-cradle hold/ pickleball hold?

---

* *The Atlantic,* "The Case Against Breast-Feeding," www.theatlantic .com/magazine/archive/2009/04/the-case-against-breast-feeding /307311.

- Can't you just pump in the bathroom stall?
- Who would ever pump in a bathroom stall?
- Isn't breastfeeding easy and relaxing?

When You Choose to Formula Feed

- Don't you know breast is best?
- Those bottles you are using are all wrong. They are too small/plastic/clear.
- Shouldn't you heat that bottle up?
- Shouldn't you cool that bottle down?
- Shouldn't that bottle be stored in a specially built chamber that is always kept at 72.5 degrees?

When You Choose to Do a Combination of Both

- Well *my* child never had a drop of formula.
- That formula will really mess up your milk supply.
- I've heard mixing formula and breast milk in a bottle increases the chances your child will want to watch *SpongeBob SquarePants* rather than *Daniel Tiger* when she is a toddler.

As you can see, everyone will have an opinion about how you should or shouldn't be feeding your child, and many of those opinions will be told directly to your face while you are attempting to feed said child. What's more, the internet has an endless supply of articles and message forums to tell you what you are doing wrong. But whatever method you choose, try to find some like-minded parents/articles/forums to ~~commiserate~~ complain about how unreasonable other people are and how you are making the right choice, no matter what that is.

Motivational Quotes for Feeding Your Baby

"Your limitation is not only in your imagination. Your child has a legitimate tongue tie that is preventing you from breastfeeding."

•

"Push yourself to tell that woman on the street that it's none of her business whether your bottle has formula or breast-milk in it, because no one else is going to do it for you."

•

"A successful place to pump at work doesn't find you, you have to go out and find it and hang a DO NOT DISTURB sign on the door."

•

"Don't wait for an opportunity to see a lactation consultant. Call them while crying so they will get you in right away."

•

"I can't give you the formula for success. But I can give you this case of formula, because it is expensive."

•

"Do one thing every day that scares you. Like breastfeeding your baby at a crowded park."

•

"Successful people were fed both formula and breastmilk as children."

•

"Don't ever stop using the excuse that your baby needs a quiet room to be in while eating. This is the secret to your getting to hide in another room during a social event."

10

Not Even Alone in Your Sleep: Managing Lack of Sleep

One of the most challenging aspects of becoming a new parent is dealing with a lack of sleep. Both my obstetrician and my son's pediatrician said they thought that parenting during the first weeks after a baby was born was harder than their medical residencies. During a residency, you know that your shift has an end time, but while parenting you never know when something will end. Babies need to be fed 5 to 20 times a night, and some will only nap while you are holding them or while they are being driven at exactly 22 miles per hour in a 2008 Toyota Corolla. Nighttime is challenging, as you'll be up to feed or soothe a baby. And when they are old enough to walk they'll scramble into your bed and try to get you to sleep like a pack of squirrels—on top of or underneath you or with some body part wedged into your back.

What's more, it's hard not to constantly compare your child against everyone else's baby. If you have a baby who doesn't sleep, then Murphy's Law says you will have a friend whose baby is lain down wide awake in their crib each night and then just coos themselves to sleep. Since my baby was not a good sleeper, I had to willfully tune out when friends with babies the same age as mine told me that their kid was already sleeping eight hours straight. When my first son was born, the initial few weeks of sleep deprivation weren't so bad. I was running on adrenaline and saw some of the upsides—I was finally up late enough to watch the end of late-night talk shows! I could binge-watch five seasons of a sitcom I had never seen! In the middle of the night, I would scroll through online baby forum message boards on my phone and commiserate with other parents who were in the same boat. But as the weeks went on and I was still up, the message boards got quieter (presumably because these people were now getting sleep) and I got more frustrated.

Some of the books I read said that newborns would spend a good portion of the day sleeping, so I entered into parenthood with some delusions about the things I would be able to get done while my baby was sleeping. But I soon learned that all babies are different and that my son was on the lower end of the "hours per day your baby should be sleeping" charts. Most of his naps were shorter than the time it takes some people to make a cup of gourmet coffee. Baby nap time also seemed to pass at approximately twice the speed of normal time.

People are also very interested in the subject of sleep—

they ask how you are sleeping or the baby is sleeping, and it can feel like your parenting is being judged if your kid is not yet sleeping well. Some people who have babies who sleep well also like to dispense advice about what you should be doing differently. Of course, it's likely you have already tried it and it did not work, or it's something you are not willing to try. The social management surrounding sleep can be almost as exhausting as the literal lack of sleep.

IF YOU HAVE A GOOD SLEEPER

Good for you! Don't brag about this to your friends whose babies aren't sleeping or try to tell them that your careful mix of Norwegian spring water, singing a specific lullaby, and tapping the baby on each foot five times before bed is the answer to all their problems. They are tired and they don't want to hear it. Just enjoy your sleep and spend your time overthinking some other important subject, like which baby bibs to buy.

IF YOU HAVE A BAD SLEEPER

You are completely in the norm. It is extremely maddening, and you are probably reading five billion articles and books on routines and methods and magic spells to help them sleep better. Some of these things may help and some may not. But hearing about how someone else's children have always been great sleepers will probably throw you into a murderous rage, so do what you need to do to block/hide/temporarily avoid those people. Those people may have parenting amnesia or are going to great lengths to paint a rosier picture of things on social media than what is going on in their real lives. Rest assured, they will encounter some other parenting challenge that you will not. There are plenty of challenges to go around.

Try to Get a Break

If you have a partner who you can trade off with, then negotiate a way to do that. If someone else can take over for you so you can sleep on the couch or in a hotel room 20 minutes from your house so you can have alone time for a little bit, then make that happen.

Reframe the Alone Time

After you finish feeding your baby at 2 a.m., instead of thinking, *I don't know how much longer I can go on doing this*, think, *I am alone in a house where everyone else is asleep, perhaps I should take a few moments to meditate or eat a bag of chips and watch* Love Is Blind. I have a friend who would use the time after her daughter woke up in the middle of the night to get a little bit of writing in. I'm typically too much of a half-asleep mess to actually do anything productive in the middle of the night, but maybe it's your chance to accomplish something.

PROBLEMS WITH COMMON ADVICE PEOPLE LIKE TO GIVE YOU

- **Sleep when the baby sleeps.** Some babies only sleep in 20-minute increments or when being pushed in a stroller by you. And it is very difficult to push a stroller in your sleep.

- **Someday you'll miss this when it's over.** Yes, you may miss the cute tiny baby fingers or moments when your baby smiles. But longing for the days when you were so tired that you washed your hair with shaving cream is probably unlikely.

- **It goes so fast.** Life with a newborn can actually go pretty slow. The first six months of my first child's life felt like it lasted approximately six years, probably because I was awake for 19 hours each day.

- **Never wake a sleeping baby.** Babies do often need to get woken so that they can eat or become slightly less nocturnal.

- **The dishes can wait.** I mean, they can wait for like a little while but unless you have some sort of magical dish cleaning elves, somebody is going to need to do them eventually. Likely you, when your baby is sleeping.

30 Totally Ridiculous Reasons Your Baby Isn't Sleeping

1. She's too hot.

2. She's too cold.

3. It's too quiet in her room.

4. The white-noise machine is keeping her up.

5. The white-noise machine is set to the wrong noise.

6. The white-noise machine you bought doesn't have the noise that would actually make her sleep.

7. She is teething.

8. She isn't teething.

9. Your baby was switched at birth and is actually sleeping great. Who knows why that baby you brought home isn't sleeping?

10. She is having a "Wonder Week."

11. She is having a "Wonder how many times I can get my parents to come into my room week."

12. She ate too much.

13. She didn't eat enough.

14. She didn't eat what that woman in the grocery store told you she fed her babies 30 years ago, back when babies never woke up at night.

15. She had a bad dream.

16. She had a good dream and wants to tell you all about it, but she can't really talk yet.

17. She needs to go to bed earlier.

18. She needs to stay up later.

19. She needs a sleep schedule.

20. She needs to sleep on demand.

21. She needs to sleep on 1,000-thread-count sheets decorated with baby chinchillas.

22. She wants you to play with her.

23. She is glad to finally have a few moments to play alone.

24. She doesn't think you really cherished every moment during the day.

25. She is getting sick.

26. She is getting sick of you trying to make her sleep all the time at night.

27. She needs her arms swaddled.

28. She wants her arms free.

29. She is trying to figure out what her arms are.

30. There is no real reason. She is just messing with you.

11

Information Overload: Dealing with Social Media and Conflicting Advice

I've had friends tell me that when they were expecting they never read books like *What to Expect When You're Expecting* because they thought that book just dispensed too much information about unlikely scenarios. I was not one of these people. Not only did I find that book very useful, but I was up late at night googling, "How much alcohol does one bite of tiramisu have in it?" I like to think things through before I do them, so I did a lot of research while I was pregnant with my first kid. Although some of the information I found was helpful, a lot of it was just contradictory or completely unrealistic. Research also always seems to change. One day a headline will be "Watching *Bubble Guppies* helps children develop social skills!" and the next day it will be, "*Bubble Guppies* will turn your child into a social outcast whose only friends are fish." Combine this with advice from other parents who insist that what worked for their kid will work for yours, and things can get overwhelming quickly.

SURVIVING SOCIAL MEDIA

I am not immune to the allure of curated parenting pictures on social media. When I see Instagram posts of sandwiches cut into the shape of hedgehogs, I sometimes think that I also want to do that, despite not having the time or artistic skills to make a cucumber look like animal fur. When I see kids in perfect poses looking at the camera instead of crying, I sometimes wonder how parents got them to do that. The answer, of course, is probably a lot of takes, bribes, and editing.

Social media is a problem because most people are living their best lives on it. A lot of people only post their own personal highlight reels, so if your kid is struggling to walk and you see someone else's child performing *Swan Lake* you are probably not going to feel very good. So, curate your feed. Keep the friends who are honest or funny and hide the ones who don't until you are in the headspace to deal with it. Same goes for celebrity parents or baby product companies trying to sell you a must-have item, like cashmere baby knee pads.

Parenting Social Media Feeds Not to Follow

- Anyone whose kids are never having a meltdown.
- Anyone whose kids can wear white clothing without visible stains.

- Anyone whose feed shows multiple pictures of kids wearing matching outfits and smiling.
- Anyone whose kids purportedly eat whatever they are given.
- Anyone claiming the product they are pushing solved a vexing parenting issue.

SURVIVING CONFLICTING EXPERT ADVICE

When my first son was born, I read approximately every baby sleep book known to humankind in an effort to get him to sleep. Some of the books were ones that my friends swore by—this was the method that turned their child into a great sleeper! But then I would try it for my son, and it wouldn't work. The books were often full of anecdotes of real parents and how they had applied the expert rules. In one of the books, a mom described a particularly difficult day of baby sleep but proudly stated at the end that she did get to take a shower that day. That was her big accomplishment—being able to take a shower. In addition to setting the bar low for what constitutes parental self-care, a lot of the books contradicted each other. Some said keep the baby up later and others said put the baby to bed at 5 p.m. Some said the pacifier must be gone by six months and others said it was fine to let a kid have one for a couple of years. People had fancy degrees and experience in the field, but they were still doling out different advice.

The problem with parenting advice is that no one-size-fits-all solution works for all the parents or kids. You should not try to be a tiger mom if you are a sloth mom, nor should you try to be an attachment parent if you don't do well with a baby clinging to your body 24/7. Once I had a second kid, I realized that the stuff that worked for the first child wouldn't necessarily work for the other. Kids are different—some have hard-set personalities or are not neurotypical. So if the baby of Jane down the street responded well to a cry-it-out technique, it doesn't mean that your kid (or you) will. Some people are good at just going with the flow or trusting their instincts, but since I live with an ongoing internal monologue, it's hard for me not to consider all the options and possibilities before acting on something. But after going down parenting information rabbit holes a few too many times, I tried to get in the habit of asking my kid's pediatrician about something first. If the answer didn't feel satisfactory, then I'd go looking for more information by consulting a reliable friend, family member, or parenting book, which was better than doing an endless internet search.

A Few Parenting Research Headlines You Will Probably Read

- Researchers Say Watching *Teletubbies* Just as Confusing for Babies as It Is for Adults.
- Study Finds New Information That Contradicts Previous Study but New Study in Works to Contradict the Contradicting Study.
- Study Finds Some Kids Who Watch Screens Have Short Attention Spans.

- Study Finds Some Kids Who Watch Screens Have Long Attention Spans.
- Study Finds Parents Who Read about Screen Research on Screens Should Probably Cut Down on Their Screen Time.
- Researchers Say Screen Time Is the Root of All Evil. Except for When It Involves Reading Books, Talking to Grandma, or Learning Another Language.
- Researchers Find Zooming with Grandma Not Actually Educational.
- Researchers Now Say Zooming with Grandma Can Be Educational if She Is Reading a Book or Teaching Quantum Physics or Something.
- Study Finds Screen Time Should Be Limited to Two Hours a Day.
- Study Finds Screen Time Should Be Limited to Zero Hours a Day.
- Researchers Say That Screen Time Should Be Restricted, Except during a Global Pandemic or on Days When a Parent Is Close to Losing Their Marbles and Then Screen Time Is Better Than Watching Mommy Destroy the Plastic Drum Set.

12

I Might Actually Be Here to Make Friends: Finding Parent Friends

While I'm not the type of person who needs a ton of friends, I do appreciate having a small group of people I can connect with. Some good friends of mine became parents around the same time I did, and it was and is helpful to have them to talk to and commiserate with. But I also found that it was useful to make new connections with parents in my neighborhood or at my children's daycare. It was nice to have some friends I knew I could talk to at the local park or daycare family picnic. Since I tend to be quiet, making new friends can be a challenge for me. But I know that introverts also often make good friends—we are good listeners, are thoughtful, and always understand if you aren't up for eating at that hip new restaurant because it is just too loud.

Making new parent friends can mean striking up conversations with strangers, something that I've always been extremely bad at doing. But I have come to realize that not all interactions with strangers are bad. If I were sitting on a plane and trying to finish a really engaging book and a stranger interrupted me to ask about what I do for a living, that would be frustrating. But if I find that that person does something similar to me or has a similar taste in books, then I'm more open to engaging with them. Studies have also found that talking with strangers can make people happier,[*] and I have had positive spontaneous interactions with strangers. So I've tried to be more open to talking with strangers, at least when I'm feeling up to it.

Some movies about moms make it look easy to have some sort of mom squad. Or at least I think that's what these mom movies feature; I haven't actually had time to watch any of them because I have kids. But in reality, making parent friends can be tough if you have trouble striking up conversations or if you have a look in public that reads to other people like, "That person does not want to talk" when in reality it is just saying, "That person wouldn't mind talking about shared interests but does not exactly know how to go about it." In some parenting spaces, it also feels like the world has already divided up into friend groups, and it can seem like a return to high school when you're trying to find the right group to fit in with. So here are some tips:

[*] NPR, "Want to Feel Happier Today? Try Talking to a Stranger," www.npr.org/sections/health-shots/2019/07/26/744267015/want-to-feel-happier-today-try-talking-to-a-stranger.

It's okay to avoid certain groups: You are probably not going to become best friends with all the other parents. If they seem to be a version of the mean girl from high school reincarnate, then they probably are a version of that mean girl, but just as a mom now.

Prepare topics: In the book *Sorry I'm Late, I Didn't Want to Come,* author Jessica Pan spends a year trying to challenge herself to do things she finds difficult as a shy introvert. She consults with experts during her journey, and one revelation I got from that book is that extroverted people sometimes do a lot of planning before social events. They think about how to connect people at a dinner party based on shared interests, or they prepare a few stories of their own ahead of time that they can use during the event. So, taking some time to prepare something to say to other parents at a preschool mixer isn't weird but an actual legitimate strategy. The book also talks about how it's better to get beyond surface level chitchat to meaningful conversations. So next time you find yourself standing next to a parent at the end of a Baby and Me class, maybe try opening with, "What's your current parenting rage level on a scale of 1 to 10?"

Talk to people who aren't talking to other people: It's intimidating to approach a group of people who are already chatting, but it's easier to talk with someone who is standing on their own pretending to read a book on their phone. This may seem obvious to some, but it took me about 30 years to figure out.

Volunteer for a position: If you have to attend an event where you don't know a lot of people, volunteer to be the one to take tickets or serve ice cream. This will give you something to do other than standing awkwardly in the corner staring at the clock.

Don't fall for MLM scams: You might get a random email from someone you sort of knew in high school who wants to have coffee to catch up. What to do? Proceed with caution. There is an 80 percent chance they are just trying to sell you nail polish strips.

MISSED CONNECTIONS FOR INTROVERTED PARENTS

- Saw you at the Baby Gym Halloween party. I appreciated how you had ironically dressed your bald baby as Lex Luthor. My child was the one carrying the baby taco costume because he refused to wear it. Do you want to be friends?

- Briefly spoke to you at the grocery store. Your child was having a meltdown because he couldn't ride the penny horse my daughter was on, and when I suggested your child could ride on the empty horse next to mine, my daughter had a meltdown. We both laughed hysterically for a while and then fled the store. Maybe we can meet up at the penny horse again next Saturday?

- You were wearing a Bon Iver shirt at the breastfeeding class that meets on Wednesdays. I was wearing a white shirt covered in coffee that I spilled on myself on the way into class. We sometimes smiled at each other while in line to weigh our babies. Do you want to meet up and discuss infant weight gain and lactation cookie recipes?

- I've been watching your posts on the anonymous parenting discussion board for over a year. You are always so measured and wise and are good at using humor to diffuse situations in a nondismissive way. Do you live near me? Do you want to get together? Are you even a real person?

- I saw you on the local mom's group Zoom meetup last Saturday and noticed some books on your bookshelf that I've also read and enjoyed. Do you want to form a book group?

- Our eyes met very briefly from time to time across the room in our baby dance class. We both shared the pained expression of people who felt they needed to get out of the house but are beginning to regret signing up for a class that forces us to dance the funky monkey in a room with a large walled mirror. Do you want to meet up sometime at a venue that does not have oversized mirrors?

- Saw you leaving the lactation room at work while I was entering, but I don't think we've ever met. Do you want to meet up after pumping next week to discuss work and form a committee to lobby for an on-site daycare?

- I got your number at the park last week because our kids got along well. I appreciated that you were brave enough to let your child have juice with high fructose corn syrup in in a public setting. My child was the one eating a cookie at 9 a.m. I want to send you a text, but I wasn't sure if you really wanted to hear from me or not. I have started several texts, but they all sounded weird. If you do want to connect, can you just be the first one to send the text?

- You were the other family with a screaming baby on the flight from Chicago to Washington, DC, last Tuesday. We stood behind you during family boarding time and joked that we were relieved there was another baby on the plane. We chose a seat near you and shared the glares of other passengers as they walked past our area searching for the farthest possible seat from us. Would you be interested in emailing me an itinerary of all the future flights you plan to take in the next year so we can book the same ones?
- I was the one who walked into the library story time a little late last Tuesday and accidentally slammed the door. When everyone turned to look at me, I just turned around and walked back out. Does anyone that was there enjoy meeting in small groups and Bon Iver? If so, send me a text.

FINDING THE VIRTUAL VILLAGE: SURVIVING PARENTING DISCUSSION GROUPS

While I'm not the type of person who will probably ever be comfortable telling a funny story to a group of people at a party, I do find it infinitely easier to tell a joke on Twitter. For me, talking via the internet is easier than talking to someone's actual face, so I've found the virtual villages that exist around parenting to be helpful. I do enjoy meeting up IRL one-on-one with other parents or in small groups, but I've also found comfort in finding the right virtual groups to connect with. For me, that has included some parenting writer groups and other general parenting groups. For you, perhaps it will be a group of parenting knitters or parents who share a phobia of creepy dolls. If you are looking for a group:

Find the right group: Some people seem to live for creating drama on social media, and groups that always devolve into a lot of fighting are probably not ideal. But finding a smaller group of people via a shared connection can offer you a lot of support and comic relief. Spending a little time lurking in a group before deciding it's for you is a solid plan.

Groups change over time: When I had my first child, I spent way too much time scrolling popular online baby forums. It helped me manage my overthinking, and it was comforting to connect with a group of people who were going through the same major life change. But after my baby was born, I spent less and less time on them and found other groups to connect with. For a while it was a group of local moms with kids the same age, and then as the kids got older that group died down too. Online parenting groups are like jeans—your tastes in them will inevitably change.

Convert online relationships to real ones: I've met a number of other writers via virtual groups that eventually led to real-life meetings at conferences or for coffee if they lived in my vicinity. Interacting in discussion groups based on our interests gave us common ground to start from. Yes, nervous before meeting them IRL, but I knew we already had a lot of common ground for topics to discuss, so I didn't even have to prepare discussion notes ahead of time.

The Rules of the Online Parenting Forum Fight Club

Welcome to the online parenting discussion board! We just have a few simple rules that we need you to agree to:

1. **You must talk about the fight club.** The nature of the fights are such that you will find yourself telling your spouse, friends, or the stranger sitting next to you at a coffee shop about how someone just posted asking if it's okay for their baby to drink a latte yet.

2. **Some posts you will think about for years to come.** You will immediately regret reading an overshare of personal details about how someone's spouse does naked yoga in front of the baby's crib every morning, and the content of that post will unfortunately be lodged in your brain for years to come.

3. **If someone tries to stop a fight, it will make it go on forever.** Trying to act in a calm and rationale manner is the wrong move on parenting discussion boards.

4. **There will never be only one fight at a time.** Our sponsors only pay us if we have at least 20 fights going at once.

5. **Shirts and shoes are optional.** You'll probably be feeding or rocking a baby while participating in the fights on your phone in the middle of the night, so there's no need to put on real clothes.

6. **Some people are just trolling.** We would kick them out, but again, our sponsors require we have at least two trolls at any given time.

7. **Certain topics will almost always lead to a fight.** If you find people behaving too civilly for a while, try posting about vaccines, pacifier use beyond the age of one, or a humblebrag about your parenting skills disguised as parenting advice.

8. **If you have just joined the message board, you must fight.** People who just lurk for the drama will be kicked out.

13

Securing Your Alone Time: Selecting Childcare

 Selecting childcare isn't something most people think about when they envision becoming a parent. But it is a big decision and poses important questions like: Would you rather confront a nanny about why she is late again or make small talk with other parents at daycare drop-off? There are a lot of factors that go into the decision for selecting childcare, including budget, safety, options in your area, and personal preferences. Selecting childcare felt like a huge undertaking to me when I had my first kid. I talked to friends, researched different options, and studied my state's childcare licensing report website like I was preparing for a college entrance exam. But one big concern you probably have is about the social demands of each of the options. Here are some things to consider:

- **Staying home to care for the child:** If you are a parent who will be staying home with a child, then one of your major considerations will be just figuring out some time when you don't have to be in charge. A top priority should be finding a way for a partner, friend, relative, or a really engaging episode of *Sesame Street* to give you a break from time to time. This option also likely involves you being the main person in charge of calling the doctor to schedule appointments and ask things like, "Should I be worried if my child just smothered butter all over his body?" So consider finding a pediatrician who lets you ask questions via email. If your partner is the one staying home with the child, just be aware that they will need many, many breaks.

- **Individual caretaker other than yourself:** Based on budget and availability, some people hire a nanny or have a trusted family member take care of their baby. If the caretaker is only caring for your offspring, then this wins you some points in the "navigating other parents" department. The downside is that you are an employer. This means you must talk to your employee about any problems that crop up. So it's important to ask yourself if you are comfortable negotiating days off for your nanny or if you have the fortitude to fire Grandma if she keeps showing up late. Some people save on costs by entering what is called a nanny share where a nanny cares for more than one family's child. I have friends for whom this arrangement worked well, but it does involve a lot of the cooks in the kitchen, which can be socially draining.

Some parents also have au pairs live with them and care for their children. For this option, you would obviously need to be willing to have another person live in your house with you. This arrangement has worked well for some people I know, and it may work particularly well for you if you happen to live in Austria, have seven children, and get an applicant who can sew clothes and teach the kids to sing and dance. Other considerations for this option include whether you work from home and how many rooms are actually in your house.

- **Childcare:** Childcare centers are another option, and they range from school-like facilities to someone's private home with one provider on duty. Bigger centers mean you won't have to scramble to find coverage when a teacher calls in sick, but this option also means you will be entering the world of managing a lot of other parents and school social situations. I had friends who had good experiences with private home daycare, but I decided that a daycare center was a better fit for me. I ended up doing a mix of days at home with me caring for my kids and other days where they were at a daycare center.

PSYCHING YOURSELF UP TO MAKE ACTUAL PHONE CALLS

I sometimes wonder how I survived growing up in an era before cell phones when text messaging wasn't an option and you had to place phone calls to a friend's house in order to talk to them. Back then, calling often involved talking to a friend's intimidating dad or grumpy sibling, which made the whole experience more difficult. Having to call people on the phone is more draining than texting or emailing for me because I never know if I'm calling at a bad time. In addition, I prefer to think through what I'm going to say, which is taxing. So I generally avoid phone calls when possible. I am often extremely grateful that I can now text or email a parent to set up a playdate for one of my kids rather than cold-calling them and stumbling through an awkward explanation about who I am and what I'm calling about. But when you are looking for childcare, you will need to call to inquire whether there are spots available and to set up tours or interviews with potential providers. So you may need some ideas to help with the calls:

- **Reward yourself:** Just like the swear jar, the reward jar can help you buy yourself something nice. Every time you successfully complete a phone call, just add a quarter or 20 to a jar. Once you have your childcare figured out, splurge on something like a new diaper bag or a night nanny.
- **Mantra:** Develop a mantra to help you to dial the number. Something like, "I can do this," or "At least I'm not a parent in the time before text messaging existed."
- **Bail out:** Try emailing, texting, or just getting someone to make some phone calls for you.

HOW TO CALL A STRANGER TO ASK ABOUT CHILDCARE

1. Locate a phone number for a childcare provider. Convince yourself it might be a cell phone number that you can text.
2. Spend several minutes composing a thoughtful text and send it to the number.
3. Cross your fingers and wait.
4. When there is no response after a while, accept that it must not be a number that takes texts.
5. Search online for an email address you can send a message to. Find none.
6. Search online for social media accounts you can send a message to. No luck.
7. Prepare to make the call. Consider the time of day. Is this the best time to call? Is it too early? Is it too late? Is it lunch time?
8. Decide you should wait.
9. An hour later, pick up the phone and dial the number.
10. Get a voice mail recording.
11. Leave a rambling message about looking for childcare.
12. Second guess whether you even managed to leave your name and number on the recording. Decide you probably did.
13. Wait.
14. See a phone call from an unknown number on your phone and let it go to voice mail.
15. Check message and realize it's the childcare provider that you will now need to call back.

16. Repeat steps 7 through 9.

17. Place another call and get someone who answers. Ask a bunch of rambling questions and then set up a time for a tour and say, "Have a good weekend!"

18. Hang up the phone and spend the rest of the after-noon thinking about how it's only Monday and you told them to have a good weekend.

FAQs about Making Phone Calls

Q My introverted partner and I are arguing over who has to call a potential childcare provider to set up a tour. How should we settle the argument?

A Make an intricate scorecard to keep track of who has done what when it comes to dreaded parent planning tasks and choose who has to call based on whoever has less points. This scorecard will also come in handy once your child arrives.

Q We don't really have time to make the scorecard right now.

A Try the following one:

Dreaded Parenting Task Scorecard

Directions: Add points for each task you complete below and keep a running tally of points to see whose turn it really is to do something.

Task	Parent 1	Parent 2
Got up with child in the middle of the night (5 points):		
Made phone call to schedule an appointment/manage some other parenting task (3 points):		
Performed emotional labor to remember something parenting-related (3 points):		
Prepared bottle/homemade baby food/other nourishment for child (3 points):		
Took child to an appointment (5 points):		
Spent the day with a sick child (7 points):		
Assembled piece of children's furniture that came in a box (10 points):		
Got up with child at 5 a.m. (4 points):		
Put child to bed (3 points):		
Watched child on own while partner went out of town (100 points):		
Running Point Tally:		

Still unsure about the best childcare option for you? Try this handy quiz:

Would you rather?

A. Have to negotiate conversations in a stay-at-home parents' playgroup.

B. Have to negotiate a salary conversation with a caretaker.

C. Have to negotiate a weekly conversation with a parent at daycare who keeps introducing himself to you like you've never met.

Are you more okay with?

A. Your child having a little extra screen time.

B. Your child sometimes wanting your nanny more than you.

C. Your child learning how hilarious the word *butt* is a little earlier than you would like.

Would you rather make small talk with?

A. Other parents at a Baby and Me class.

B. A babysitter.

C. A preschool teacher.

Your tolerance for noise level in your own home is?

A. Manageable, and you own earplugs.

B. Okay if it's being kept in a separate room of the house and managed by someone else.

C. Not great. The sound of "The Wheels on the Bus" on repeat from three rooms away makes you want to smash things.

If you are unhappy with your current childcare provider, would you rather?

A. Have a talk with yourself about self-care.

B. Fire a nanny/grandma.

C. Make up some excuse about how you are moving to another country and then switch your child to a care center on the other side of town.

Mostly As: Stay-at-home parenting may be for you.

Mostly Bs: Nanny time.

Mostly Cs: Look into your local learnin' academies.

14

Required Outings: Managing Doctor Visits

 On our first visit to the pediatrician after my oldest son was born, they put us in an exam room to wait for our doctor. As my husband and I sat with our mostly quiet baby, we could hear a series of noises getting louder from the room next to us that sounded like a wild animal had gotten loose— there was crying and screaming and a series of crashes that I'm still not sure what they were. Whenever I take my kids to the pediatrician now, I think of that visit to assure myself that things could always be going worse. Taking a small human to the doctor is challenging because there is often a lot of waiting around, meaning that your parenting skills will be on display for the staff and parents in the waiting room. There is a 90 percent chance your child will cry at least once during the visit, and you must try to look like you have got things together even though you may not.

When you have a baby, you will be seeing the doctor a lot—the pediatrician for checkups and illness checks, and your obstetrician for postpartum checks. Not to mention potential visits to a variety of therapists and lactation consultants that both you and your small bundle of screams may need to go to. As an added bonus, you're also supposed to start visiting the dentist in your child's first year of life so they can get an early start on talking to your baby about flossing. Successfully taking a child to a medical visit can take a week or two of recovery time.

MANAGING DOCTOR VISITS

Choose telemedicine: Some doctors offer the option for you to video chat with them rather than to visit in person. The former is often much easier to manage since you can keep your child entertained with a pacifier and episode of *Elmo's World* off-screen until your doctor is ready. Just make sure to mute the video when the doctor shows up onscreen.

Go prepared: If you have to go to a physical appointment, you should prepare to bring a baby in roughly the same way a carefree college student prepares for a European vacation—by packing a lot of outfits and electronic devices to keep yourself entertained.

Change doctors: It requires a lot of effort and phone calls, but if you aren't really jibing with the doctor you chose, and your insurance and geographic situation allow for it, find a new one.

Realistic Steps to Visiting the Doctor with a Baby

1. Assemble a suitcase-sized diaper bag with burp cloths, blanket, wipes, pacifiers, and a lot of snacks for yourself.
2. Strap child into their car seat and secure to car or stroller.
3. Travel to doctor's office. Baby immediately falls asleep. Perfect! Hopefully baby will nap contentedly until visit.
4. Arrive at doctor's office and bring in the sleeping child in the car seat. Sit down in the waiting area for two minutes before a toddler in the waiting area throws themselves on the floor and starts screaming.
5. Your baby wakes up and joins in the screaming.
6. Try not to curse toddler too much since in a couple of years your child will be a toddler who does the same thing.
7. While baby is still screaming, get called back to the exam room and smile at the nurse through gritted teeth.
8. Take baby to the exam room where there is a giant mirror. Baby notices the baby in the mirror and stops crying. Remove baby's clothes and diaper so child can be weighed. Baby immediately pees everywhere.
9. Clean up pee and weigh child.

10. Go to get fresh diaper and realize diapers are the one thing you did not pack in your diaper bag.

11. Gratefully accept diaper from nurse.

12. Nurse leaves room and baby starts to scream.

13. Try to determine if crying is "tired cry," "hungry cry," or "I'm naked at a strange place under a bunch of fluorescent lights and I don't understand why cry."

14. Determine all cries sound the same.

15. Try to do some shushing and swinging so that when doctor arrives you will not look like a completely incompetent parent.

16. Pull out pacifier. Baby spits it out onto the floor. Rinse pacifier off and put it in your bag.

17. Doctor arrives and baby stops crying. Doctor examines child and explains that the dot on child's leg is not rare skin rash you saw on the internet but just a birthmark.

18. Thank doctor and get baby dressed.

19. Baby immediately has a blowout.

20. Undress baby and accept fresh diaper from the doctor.

21. Get baby dressed and go home. Collapse on the couch for a week.

AGES AND STAGES FOR INTROVERTED PARENTS

Parents—gauge how well you are doing on parenting milestones by responding "Yes," "Sometimes," or "No" for each of the following questions:

Communication Skills

A. Do you say hello to parents you don't know?

B. Are you still thinking about the awkward thing you said to your Baby and Me swim instructor two months ago?

C. Do you use your baby as an excuse to avoid small talk?

D. Do you talk more than your baby?

Gross Motor Skills

A. When you see another parent you know at the grocery store, how quickly can you avoid them without having them see you?

B. Can you stay in a crouching position for at least 20 minutes to avoid your neighbor who always ropes you into a lengthy conversation?

Problem Solving

A. If you are invited to a kid's birthday party, can you invent a believable reason for not being able to attend?

B. If a baby play gym is getting too loud, can you locate the exit in under five seconds?

Personal-Social

A. Do you smile at other parents yet?

B. Are you able to make eye contact with others for longer than half a second?

15

How to Deal with
Never Being Alone

When I was pregnant with my first child, I started reading about different parenting styles and stumbled onto attachment parenting—an approach that potentially has parents keep babies with them all day and night. Some people hear about this style and think it sounds like a nourishing and plausible way to raise a child. When I heard about it, I thought that there is no way I could do that because I would never be alone. If you are the type of person who draws energy from getting alone time, parenting will tap into the well of your energy and pump it dry. When you become a parent, you realize that it is very hard to be alone. Sure, your baby is unlikely to engage you in boring small talk, but trying to keep a small human alive 24/7 can be draining, even with the good moments mixed in. Even if you aren't opting for attachment parenting, you will still be spending most of the day and a good part of the night with a tiny person, and any alone time you can get will have to be negotiated with a spouse, partner, or sitter. What's more, if you have a spouse or partner, you will also be spending a lot of time with that person, and even though they are probably very lovely, you may also need a break from them at times. When you become a parent, things that used to feel like a chore (like your commute or a trip to the grocery store) become enjoyable mini vacations that you can have without toting a baby along.

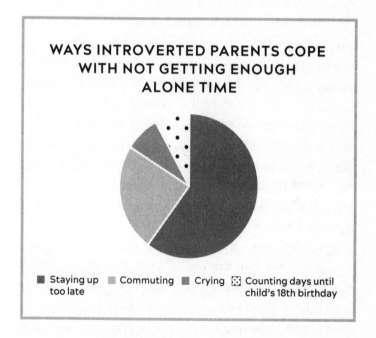

WAYS INTROVERTED PARENTS COPE WITH NOT GETTING ENOUGH ALONE TIME

■ Staying up too late   ■ Commuting   ■ Crying   ⊠ Counting days until child's 18th birthday

WAYS TO GET SOME ALONE TIME

When the baby sleeps: Sleep is one way to gain some solitude. If you are the only one in the house when the baby naps (and the baby is not napping directly on your body), then you will get a little alone time. The problem is that although you might technically be alone, you will probably be trying to do laundry or eat something or take a super stressful light nap while you try to listen for the baby to wake up. Of course, you will also get some alone time when you are asleep. So perhaps the ultimate time for quiet time is in your dreams. You know, as long as they aren't anxiety nightmares about how you have to complete a math final while also caring for a baby.

Staying up too late: In an ideal world, you would go to sleep shortly after your baby does because you are probably exhausted. But one of the best ways to get alone time is to stay up late. If you have a significant other who likes to do this too, you can just choose one of the escape options outlined later in this chapter to get your alone time, or you can play a game of who can stay up the latest to score a few more minutes of alone time/pain from loss of sleep the next day.

Get a babysitter: It can be hard and expensive to get a babysitter when a baby is young; plus, you would probably like to spend several months evaluating dozens of caregivers and carefully weighing the pros and cons to each of them before selecting one. But you will have to toss some of that overthinking out and just get someone who is responsible enough to keep your kid alive for a bit, so you can get out of the house alone to wander the frozen food aisles of the grocery store.

Lean on friends and family members who like to hold babies: Some people are kind of obsessed with holding babies. They are the ones always offering to hold the baby so you can eat when they come to visit. If you have friends or family members who are like this, ask them to come over and hold the baby so you can pretend to go to the grocery store but instead just sit in your parked car listening to an audiobook.

Procure whatever baby equipment works to buy you some time to take a shower or eat a meal two-handed: Is a baby space pod worth $200 if it allows you to take a shower? Yes. Especially if you can consign it when you are done with it. Or see what equipment you can borrow from friends and family members so that you can enjoy your precious moments of alone time.

Go back to work: As long as you don't work as a Walmart greeter or door-to-door salesperson, your job is likely to provide you a few moments of reprieve from people at least some of the time.

Walks: Most babies are happy to be put in a stroller and pushed around the block or the neighborhood. Even though you are not technically alone while pushing a stroller, it can feel like you are somewhat alone, especially if the child is sleeping or sucking on a pacifier that some parents are silently judging you for letting your child have.

Take full advantage of Hallmark holidays: The true gift for any new parent is time away from their kids, so take full advantage of the holiday of your choice (Mother's Day, Father's Day, National Taco Day) and insist on celebrating it with something like a spa day or a European vacation while someone else watches your child.

Travel Reviews of Everyday Parent Getaways

Closet: ★ ★
I like that this is a less likely hiding spot than other rooms and that there are several located throughout the house. But the space in these getaways is typically small since they are literally closets.

Bathroom: ★ ★
The floor is kind of uncomfortable to sit on, but I appreciate that this getaway has a well-functioning lock and offers a built-in excuse for being in there for at least a little while each day. But once my kid got a little bigger and learned how to walk and pound on doors, it started to feel less like a spa and more like being trapped in a zombie horror movie hideout.

The gym: ★ ★ ★
This place has a childcare area and a good assortment of snacks in the vending machine. Most people are also too busy focusing on their own workouts to notice that I just come to the gym to read a book and eat Red Vines in the locker room. I just wish they would extend the childcare time to longer than two hours and maybe let you occasionally leave the building.

Laundry room: ★ ★ ★
I've been spending a lot of time at this spartan oasis lately. I like that I can multitask by folding clothes while I'm there, but the noises at all hours of the day and night can be annoying.

Pumping gas: ★ ★
I know it only gives me a few minutes of alone time, but I find that pumping gas is an effective way to gain a few minutes of time to recharge. I can see my kid in their car seat the whole time, but I can't hear them yelling when a cracker just broke in half.

Standing near an open window in my own home: ★ ★ ⯪
The fresh air is refreshing and I like nibbling on the complimentary cheese and crackers while gazing outside. But the odds of guests staying nearby who want to stop and chat with me like I was at some sort of B&B happy hour doesn't make this option the perfect escape.

Under the bed: ★ ★ ★ ⯪
Not the best hiding spot when you've got a crawling baby, but this getaway is great for parents of slightly older children, especially if their kids are afraid of monsters.

Commute: ★ ★ ★ ★
Before having kids, this was a stress-inducing part of my day. I couldn't wait to get home so I could relax and unwind. Now that I have kids, the time alone in the car listening to podcasts is my moment of Zen before returning home. Sometimes I purposely drive directly into a traffic jam just to get a little more me time.

Hotel room: ★ ★ ★ ★ ★
The room might be a little dated and the wall of dream

catchers might be a little strange, but I barely notice it because I get eight solid hours of sleep and spend the rest of the time lying in bed watching TV. I plan to do this frequently, as the hotel is only a short distance from my house.

16

The Days Are Long, but the Baby Classes Are Longer: Surviving Parent-Child Classes

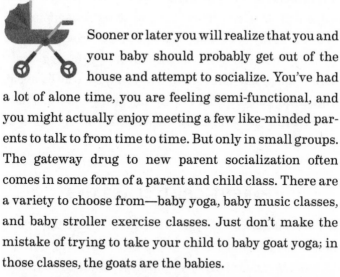Sooner or later you will realize that you and your baby should probably get out of the house and attempt to socialize. You've had a lot of alone time, you are feeling semi-functional, and you might actually enjoy meeting a few like-minded parents to talk to from time to time. But only in small groups. The gateway drug to new parent socialization often comes in some form of a parent and child class. There are a variety to choose from—baby yoga, baby music classes, and baby stroller exercise classes. Just don't make the mistake of trying to take your child to baby goat yoga; in those classes, the goats are the babies.

One of the first parent-child classes that I attended was a music class. I had heard good things about it from other parents and I thought my kid might enjoy it. What I didn't realize was that gathering a group of infants to five-year-olds in a class with caregivers, who themselves have a range of styles, could be chaotic. There was a lot of random hitting and biting, and there were at least five tantrums per class over who got to use one of the coveted tambourines. To the instructor's credit, he ran a pretty tight ship and was not afraid to call kids out when they were trying to use the drums as a trampoline. But I learned that I still needed to navigate interactions with the other participants. At the first class we attended, one kid grabbed the egg maraca my kid had been using. I wasn't quite sure what to do—the parent of the grabber was sitting next to me and saw it happen but didn't say anything. Should I just grab it back? Should I ask her to ask her child to give it back, or was that overstepping my bounds? If my kid wasn't that upset, did it really matter? Luckily, the grabby kid quickly dropped the egg, and I solved the problem in a completely mature way by avoiding sitting next to that family in future classes. That's when I realized that these classes were not going to be very relaxing.

PARENT-CHILD CLASS TIPS

Choose your class wisely: If you do not deal with loud noises very well, then try to choose something smaller or quieter. There will be children screaming no matter what class you take, but your goal is also not to endure a bunch of extra noise that the li'l drummers class would provide.

Find something close to home: Spending an hour driving back and forth from a class that is supposed to turn your baby into Van Gogh will not be worth it in more ways than one.

Don't overload your schedule: Some parents start overscheduling their children roughly a week after they enter the world, but overloading will probably only stress you out, so just try one class at time.

Get recommendations from like-minded friends: Your extroverted friend may have enjoyed the Baby and Me musical theater production class, but I'm guessing you will not.

PROS AND CONS TO DIFFERENT CLASSES

Music Class

Pro: Your child may enjoy the music and interaction with other kids.

Con: Jingle sticks can be used as weapons.

Stroller Exercise

Pro: People will be too busy trying to breathe to make very much small talk.

Con: Your child will eventually outgrow the stroller and will want to push it around instead of letting you do your leg lifts.

Baby Yoga

Pro: It's mellow and quiet.
Con: Some super yoga mom will inevitably be doing a headstand while breastfeeding her twins.

Storytime

Pro: It's free and usually at a library, which is supposed to be quiet.
Con: Everyone will stare at you when your child has a meltdown over not being able to chew on a book.

EXIT STRATEGIES WHEN YOU REALIZE YOU ARE IN THE WRONG CLASS

- Lift your baby up and smell their diaper. Make a face, collect your things, leave, and then never come back.
- Develop a secret code you can text to a friend that means they should immediately call you when they get it. Then take the call and talk loudly about how you will of course be there right away.
- Bring a large blanket to hide under and pretend you are invisible for the rest of the class. Everyone will probably be relieved when you don't come back after that.

17

Birthday Parties: Throwing Them

The first birthday party you throw for a child can be exhausting. Some people plan their kid's birthday parties in the same way they would a wedding—complete with catering, custom-ordered outfits, and Instagrammable smash cakes. I was one of those parents who bought first-birthday-party smash cakes because they seemed cute, and Pinterest sometimes puts some sort of inexplicable magic spell on me. But one of my kids was too overwhelmed by all the people singing "Happy Birthday" while staring at him to eat the cake, and he mostly just stared at the pricey cake and cried (an early sign that he is probably an introvert).

Getting through the first year of parenthood did feel like a big accomplishment worth celebrating to me. It's pretty amazing to watch a child go from a tiny baby that fits snugly on your lap to a one-year-old who can get around on their own, so I didn't want to skip celebrating the milestone. Luckily, when your child is young, they don't really know what a birthday is. Chances are they will be much more interested in playing with the wrapping paper and box the present came in rather than the $50 set of sustainably sourced educational wooden blocks. Throwing the party yourself gives you complete control over the party plans and guest list, and you can try to keep things more manageable.

PRE-PARTY MANTRAS

- This only happens once a year.
- Only 17 more of these more to host.
- Just remember, nothing ends a party faster than turning on the soundtrack to *PAW Patrol*.
- The party is at my home, and I'll hide if I want to.

THE BASICS

Location: As your child gets older, it's often preferable to pay an exorbitant amount of money to some party-hosting location to host a party for you—they will do the prep and cleaning and feed and entertain the kids, and you can fade into the background. But birthdays at home are often better for younger kids, and one upside is that if people haven't left by nap time, you can hide in another room for an hour while you put your child down for a nap/take your own nap.

The guest list: Try to keep the guest list manageable to the number of people you want to host. If you aren't dreading the idea of making small talk with them, then it's probably safe to invite them.

Food: Cleaning and prepping for a party can be overwhelming as it is, but trying to do it while operating on little sleep and entertaining a kid can feel impossible. If you enjoy making certain foods or cake, then go for it. Managing food prep during a party can also allow you to focus on something other than the bad job of socializing that you are doing, so it can be a good way to occupy yourself. But if overseeing food is going to stress you out, and your budget allows it, just order prepared food.

The timing: Work around nap times and keep it short. Your kid(s) will have a meltdown at some point during the party no matter what you do, but choosing the right timing may help you from melting down too.

Smash cakes: Are cute on Instagram, but have a 50/50 chance of making your child burst into tears. Still, embrace it if you are into it (like I was).

Music: Nothing too loud or with the lyrics *baby, little,* or *hokey pokey* in them.

FIRST BIRTHDAY PARTY THEME IDEAS

Costume party: You can wear a mask and literally hide in plain sight.

Silent birthday party: Just like a silent disco, but with less dancing.

Spaceship party: Set up lots of spaceship structures that anyone can hide in for a little bit.

Introvert party: Everyone celebrates! Separately, in their own homes.

PART THREE

WELCOME TO
TODDLERVILLE

18

Forced Socialization: Playdates

 Sooner or later, your child will probably be invited for a playdate. Great! You may think, "I'll just drop off my kid at someone else's house and get some alone time." Unfortunately, that won't work when you have a young child. You, too, will have to attend and participate in the playdate. The world of playdates can be stressful because it involves you chatting with another parent or caregiver who you don't know well. This can potentially lead you into a minefield of parenting issues that include discipline, how clean you keep your house, and whether you only let organic, locally sourced, no-dye cheese puffs near your child. When taking my child on a playdate to a new house, I usually get stressed out if I walk into what appears to be a photoshoot for *Better Homes & Gardens*. On the other hand, if I see some unmade beds and toys strewn about, I can relax.

Getting playdate timing right is also tricky because toddlers can nap at different times of day, leaving only a few brief windows when everyone isn't hungry or tired. Even if you do hit a window of golden timing, sometimes kids will show little interest in playing with each other during the carefully orchestrated meeting time. Playdates can also involve negotiating siblings, pets, and children who are at an age where they like to periodically whip their pants off. It's basically like trying to negotiate a corporate merger between very eccentric CEOs.

Still, sometimes playdates can lead to you forming genuine bonds with another family, and your child will probably benefit from some socializing, so making yourself set up one every six months isn't a bad idea.

IMPORTANT LOCATION CONSIDERATIONS

Your house: This is an okay option because you have some control over the situation, and if your toddler grabs an expensive figurine and smashes it, you only have yourself to blame. But you will also potentially have to clean your house. What's more, if someone is visiting your home, it can be hard to get them to leave when you feel that it is time.

Other people's house: This is one of the most stressful options when you don't know the people. Do they bother with baby gates, or not? Do they keep out the toys that their kid is possessive about? If so, are you prepared for the inevitable playdate war? Are they going to make you engage in super-energetic tag games with the children instead of just letting you sit at the table and sip coffee?

Virtual playdates: If a friend lives far away or there is a global pandemic, then your child may be asked to a virtual playdate—where they video chat with their friends instead of meeting IRL. These playdates require minimal effort on your part, are considered one of the less evil forms of screen time, and when you're ready for the playdate to be over you can always claim the battery on your device is about to die. So they are pretty great.

Other locations: Sometimes it's easiest to meet in a mutually agreed upon neutral location for a playdate. A park or play area gives kids a place to hang out, plus there is nature and birds and stuff.

POTENTIAL PLAYDATE PROBLEMS AND SOLUTIONS

- **Problem:** Your child is an extrovert and wants to have a playdate approximately once every hour.

  Solution: Take your child on playdates occasionally. Strongly encourage them to play with imaginary friends the rest of the time.

- **Problem:** Your child wants to have a playdate with another child, but you aren't exactly clicking with their parent(s).

  Solution: Sign up your child for a class with the other child. Preferably one that allows you to hide in the corner most of the time.

- **Problem:** A family keeps dropping by unexpectedly for impromptu playdates.

  Solution: Install a doorbell camera or hang a sign that says: NO UNSOLICITED PLAYDATES.

- **Problem:** You are hosting a playdate that has gone on for a couple of hours but are getting pretty worn out and need it to end.

  Solution: Do whatever it takes to get your toddler to have a meltdown.

- **Problem:** Before a playdate, parenting experts recommend you ask about body safety rules, pets in the house, weapons in the house, allergies, vaccinations, and for a laminated list of every illness that all members of the household have experienced in the past six months, but you aren't sure how to bring up half of the subjects.

  Solution: Develop a playdate screening questionnaire. Here are some questions to get you started.

Playdate Screening Questionnaire

Save everyone some time by having families fill out this helpful screening questionnaire before a playdate, and then use the answers to decide if you will be a good fit!

When hosting a playdate, I like to:

A. Set up a strict schedule of play/snack/craft time that we must stick to.

B. Get everyone involved in staging an elaborate production of *Seussical,* the musical.

C. Dump some Duplo bricks on the floor and turn on *Bluey.*

My idea of a perfect day is:

A. A loud Zumba class and taking my kids to a bouncy house gym that blasts pop music.

B. Hosting a dinner party for 20 people I've just met.

C. My kid falls asleep by 7 p.m. and I get to concentrate on *The Great British Baking Show* for two solid hours.

How would you describe how clean your house is?

A. The beds are made every day and the children cheerfully clean up their messes at the end of each day.

B. A little messy here or there, but not too bad.

C. Sort of like hoarders, but with toys.

Snacks at my home:

A. Are always organic and locally sourced and only come in earth tones.

B. Include some healthy options, but my kids can have sugar sometimes.

C. Are whatever I could buy in bulk at Costco.

In terms of safety in my home:

A. I am basically the Marie Kondo of keeping unsafe things out of my house.

B. I've got some baby gates up, but I can't guarantee all the plastic toys are BPA-free.

C. Safety? I don't really worry about stuff that is unlikely to happen.

The toys in my home are:

A. Wooden and educational.

B. Plastic, but entertaining.

C. Loud.

At playdates my child tends to:

A. Demand that whoever they are playing with play the same thing.

B. Cry.

C. Hide in their room the whole time. There is some chance you won't even see them!

19

Attending Kids' Birthday Parties

As soon as your child is born, they will start getting invited to birthday parties. Some particularly hip babies may also get invites in utero. Long before a baby is old enough to eat cake or whack open a piñata, they will be expected to attend birthday parties. Unfortunately, it's commonly frowned upon for you to show up at a party, drop a baby off, and say you'll be back in two hours to pick them up. So, you must go too. And if your kid can't talk yet, guess who will be covering the small talk at the party? That's right, you.

I tend to get stressed out if my weekend is completely booked with activities, because I need some down time to recover from the busyness and socializing during the week. Having something on my schedule that holds me to a set time also generates some low level of anxiety, because I get concerned that I am going to somehow miss it. When my kids hit a certain age, it seemed like we were managing a birthday party invite almost every weekend. Attending a party involved a lot of stressing out about what to buy as a present and what parent socializing at the party would be like. Not attending a party could bring additional stresses about whether I turned down an invitation to a party for a kid my child was actually friends with.

By the time your child is a preschooler, you will probably be invited to all-class parties. If you have two or more kids, the numbers grow exponentially. Assuming you can't drop a kid off until they are at least 6, and possibly until they are 15, you will be expected to attend a mind-numbing number of children's birthday parties. Don't even try to calculate the number, it will only make you sad. Given all this, you will need some survival tips.

PRE-PARTY OPTIONS

Just say no: Parenthood comes with a million built-in excuses, and modern parents love to overschedule. If you get a party invite and you really don't want to attend, simply explain that little Emma's parkour class is scheduled at that time and you can't let her miss out on it.

Lean into illness: When you have young kids, someone in the household is likely to be sick approximately 99 percent of the time, and most people are more than happy to have you cancel if you or your child has sneezed sometime in the last month.

KIDS' BIRTHDAY PARTIES YOU WILL BE INVITED TO

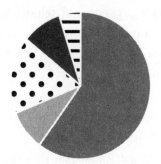

■ Kids your kid once had a class with	■ Family members you are not even sure you are really related to	⬚ People you once worked with who now have kids	■ Random kids your kid befriended on the street	☰ It's unclear how you know them, but you got an invite so you might have to go

Send an extroverted caretaker in your place: Do you have a partner, grandparent, or friendly looking neighborhood barista who might be able to take your kid to the party and enjoy it? If so, let them. You can just stay home and binge Netflix. After all, you probably haven't seen a movie in three years.

Commit to only attending a certain number of parties per year: You probably can't feasibly say yes to all the parties your kids will be invited to, and truth be told some people who invite the whole class are really counting on there being a lot of people who can't attend. So do everyone a favor and decline invitations. Decide on a reasonable amount of parties to attend and then go to the ones for kids who your kid actually seems to be friends with, that involve a friend or family member you are looking forward to catching up with, or that are extremely short.

DURING PARTY SURVIVAL STRATEGIES

Couldn't get out of the party altogether? Here are some helpful survival strategies:

Arrive late: It's a well-known fact that leaving the house with kids is like capturing an octopus in the ocean and trying to stuff it into a goldfish bowl. Take advantage of this and arrive about 15 minutes before the party is about to end.

Use your kid: Having a kid at a party is kind of good when you aren't super social. You always have someone to talk to—your kid! Sure, they may be busy playing with other kids, but then you can always go over to "check on them." If your child is still a baby, you can always pinch them a little to make them cry and then announce, "Well, it looks like we have overstayed our welcome!" Parents who escort screaming children out of parties are rarely chastised.

Act oddly to ward off future invitations: Why not try showing up to the party in a creepy clown costume? Or just corner some parents and try to sell them a time-share.

Prepare: Introverts like to be prepared, so before attending a party, go through this prep list.

Children's Birthday Party Survival Prep List

During the party, I will:

____ Hide in the bathroom.

____ Hide outside, pretending I'm on an important call.

____ Sit in the back of a room and read a book.

If loud grating music comes on, I will:

____ Put in my own earbuds and listen to something calming.

____ Sneak over to the source of the music and turn it down.

____ Sit near another parent who looks to be visibly pained by the party experience.

Conversation topics that will make me retreat to one of my hiding spots:

____ Possible colleges for our four-year-olds.

____ The weather.

____ How to hire the clown at the party.

Things that will make me immediately leave the party:

____ Parents required to participate in dancing.

____ Karaoke.

____ Tommy's dad.

Things I can do to relieve stress while at the party:

____ Listen to a meditation app.

____ Squeeze on a stress ball.

____ Take a turn hitting the piñata.

Children's Birthday Party Survival Prep List *(continued)*

Prepared conversation topics to write on my hand before going in:

____ Which gyms have drop-off childcares *and* are also located next to nice restaurants to get lunch.

____ Kids' TV shows that make them want to gouge their eyes out.

____ Kids' TV shows that don't make them want to gouge their eyes out.

____ The location and condition of active construction sites around town that are easily viewable for small children.

____ Elementary schools that require the least amount of door-to-door selling fundraisers.

AFTER-PARTY CELEBRATION IDEAS

It's key to #treatyoself after you have survived attending another child's birthday party. Here are some ideas:

Food treats: Give yourself a small treat as a reward—perhaps a cookie or a rented chocolate fountain.

Drinkable treats: After your child is in bed, sip a cocktail or some top-shelf chamomile.

Post-party mantra: Perhaps the treat you need is mental reassurance. So you could develop a post-party mantra like, "You did it—it wasn't that bad," or "One party down, only 20 more to go this year."

20

All Eyes on You: Public Tantrums

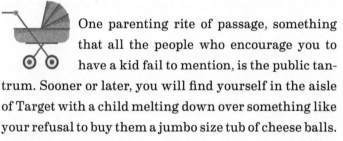 One parenting rite of passage, something that all the people who encourage you to have a kid fail to mention, is the public tantrum. Sooner or later, you will find yourself in the aisle of Target with a child melting down over something like your refusal to buy them a jumbo size tub of cheese balls.

When my kids were young, we went to a local Vietnamese restaurant to have dinner. We got a table and sat down, and then my youngest proceeded to have an epic meltdown that could not be reversed. Since the restaurant was small and it didn't look like we could turn things around, we left before ordering and then avoided going to that restaurant for a year or two. Once my kids were a bit older, we did start going back. Some illogical part of my brain wondered if this epic meltdown was somehow still remembered by the staff, but the staff was actually extremely nice and sometimes seemed happier to see the kids at my table than the adults (of course, this is something extremely rare in the world of dining out with children). So, yes, you will always remember your child's epic meltdowns, but luckily, the rest of the public probably will not.

QUICK TANTRUM TIPS

Know you're not alone: All kids have meltdowns at some point or another. At times, when one of my kids was melting down in public, another parent has come up and told me about an epic meltdown their kid had. Turns out, this is much more helpful than just snapping a picture of the scene and posting it to Facebook.

Avoid leaving the house: If you can't leave the house because of potty training or a local stay-at-home order, then it is basically impossible to have a public tantrum. Of course, it will still be possible to have an at-home tantrum that the neighbors may overhear, but you can't win them all.

Avoid shopping close to home: Meltdowns can be easier if they are only witnessed by people who you will never see again. There are just too many chances to run into someone you know at your local grocery store.

Master quick exits: The best solution to a meltdown is to leave the scene as quickly as possible. So pick up the child, abandon the cart, and get out of there, and don't go back for a couple of years.

Prepare a note to hand to strangers that throw you judging looks: It could say something like, "Luckily this was only five minutes of your life, imagine if you were living it every day."

CELEBRITIES WHOSE KIDS HAVE HAD EPIC MELTDOWNS

When your child is throwing a tantrum in the middle of the grocery store checkout line, you can take some comfort in the fact that at least you are not a celebrity and the tantrum is less likely to be filmed and sold to a gossip website. (If you are a celebrity who happens to be reading this, then thank you; I love your work, and I'm sorry about the constant scrutiny of your parenting.) But take comfort in the fact that celebrities are just like us. Here are just a few of the child meltdowns of the famous:

- **Drew Barrymore's child at Disney.** Drew's daughter had meltdowns at both Disney World and Disneyland. So when you take your child to a theme park and they start screaming when their pretzel doesn't have enough salt on it, know that it isn't just you.[*]
- **Actor Justin Baldoni's toddler at Whole Foods.**[†] When Baldoni's daughter threw herself on the floor of a Whole Foods in 2017, he posted about it on Instagram and was

---

[*] *E!*, "Drew Barrymore's Daughter Olive Has a Meltdown at Disney World," www.eonline.com/news/828194/drew-barrymore-s-daughter-olive-has-a-meltdown-at-disney-world#.

[†] Bustle, "Why This Dad's Post about His Daughter's Tantrum Is Going Viral," www.bustle.com/p/this-dads-viral-post-on-ignoring-his-daughters-public-tantrum-is-shifting-important-narrative-in-parenting-66917.

very cool and chill about the whole thing. So if you can somehow channel this when your own child is losing it, then you should be nominated for a parenting award.

- **Kim Kardashian and Kanye West's child North West.** North has been photographed having meltdowns in a variety of locations including at a fashion show, a fancy restaurant, and in her mom's closet when she couldn't wear her fancy shoes. So even if you had access to a lot of fancy things, your child would still have tantrums.

CHERISH EVERY MOMENT WITH YOUNG KIDS—OR NOT

People with parenting amnesia sometimes like to tell parents of young kids to "cherish every moment." But not all parenting moments are ones that you need to enjoy.

- Cherish some moments, but not the ones when your child is screaming at the top of their lungs over having to put on pants.
- Cherish the moments when your child is willing to wear pants.
- Don't cherish every moment of parenting a baby with colic.
- Do cherish the moment when the colic seems to have finally passed.
- Don't cherish the times when someone who has an unusually well-behaved baby tells you all the things you should be doing differently with yours.
- Do cherish the moment when a know-it-all parent has

another baby who does not behave quite as well as their first.

- Cherish the moment when you first throw in the towel and let your kid watch *Dinosaur Train* and you get to lie on the couch uninterrupted for a full 10 minutes.
- Cherish the day you get your toddler to eat kale.
- Don't cherish the moment, two days later, when your toddler declares they will no longer eat kale.
- Cherish the time when your child threw a tantrum in Target, and no one stopped to tell you to cherish that moment.
- Cherish every garden gnome ornament you see. Those things are cute.
- Don't cherish all the messages posted to online parenting boards from people who think they have the answer on how to get your child to sleep/eat/behave like a French baby.
- Cherish the time when you realize the person who just told you to "cherish every moment" probably has selective amnesia brought on by years of sleep deprivation from when their children were young.
- Cherish every parent friend who is honest with you and admits that they are not loving every minute of raising kids.
- Cherish some moments, but if someone offers to extract a few of the others in some sort of *Eternal Sunshine of the Spotless Mind* scenario, definitely ask for more details.
- Cherish the evenings when you get to read your favorite books to your child while they are snuggled up in your arms.

- Don't cherish the moments your kid keeps insisting you read that book with the unpronounceable dinosaur names.
- Cherish the moment you realize the dinosaur book can be hidden under your bed.
- Don't cherish the moment when your child is playing hide and seek, hides under your bed, and discovers the dinosaur book and insists you read it every day for the next month.
- Don't cherish the time when your child keeps getting out of bed in some sort of never-ending *Groundhog Day* scenario.
- Do cherish the moment when your child goes to bed for real.
- Do cherish the moment when you sneak back into your kid's room to reassure yourself that your child is still sleeping/breathing, avoid accidentally waking them up, and then sneak back downstairs to watch *Nailed It!* and eat cupcakes.
- Cherish the moment when an older relative tells you that they really hated some aspects of parenting.
- Cherish every whimsical MoMA art exhibit that your kids delight in. Those experiences can be pretty great.
- Don't cherish the first time you googled a picture of Momo. That thing is scary.
- Cherish the moments when you envision yourself in the future not telling stressed-out new parents to cherish every moment.

21

Kids Are Loud: Trying to Find Your Quiet

Kids are loud. When you have a baby, they will cry. And to prevent the child from crying more, you may find yourself vacuuming or blasting "The Wheels on the Bus" in the car on the regular. If you have more than one kid, they will spend some time fighting or yelling or singing "Let It Go" on repeat for several years. Before becoming a parent, you may think, "Oh, I'm not going to be one of those parents who blasts annoying kids music in the car—my baby will grow up listening to cool indie bands and never want that other music." But that will go out the window the first time you drive to a doctor's appointment in a sleep-deprived state while your baby screams at the top of his lungs for some unknown reason. So you'll fold and turn on the Mickey Mouse Clubhouse "Hot Dog!" because at least it is performed by They Might Be Giants, and they have some sort of indie cred. And soon you'll realize that you can often just tune out the music. Soon after I became a parent I started putting on some kid music in the car to survive driving trips. Then when I started dropping off my kids at day care, I would sometimes accidentally leave the music on and listen to it for 20 minutes before realizing I was on my own and did not need to subject myself to a rousing rendition of "Heads, Shoulders, Knees, and Toes" anymore.

The noise level in your life will rise not only while transporting your child places but also in your home and while in public. Because my husband and I are pretty laid-back people, I think I imagined that my kids would be mellow. *They will just hang out and read books and teach themselves cursive or something,* I naively thought. But both of my kids are very active and often loud. It is a truth universally acknowledged that if you are a parent who is particularly sensitive to loud or constant noises, then figuring out a way to get some quiet time is important.

WAYS TO GET SOME QUIET

Naps: Naps are the ideal time to get some quiet during the day. If you have only one child who reliably takes a nap, then cherish every moment of alone time you get when they sleep. You can use nap time to check off some items on your to-do list or perform some form of self-care like scrolling social media and drinking soda. But some kids don't nap well. And if you have multiple kids, then getting them on the same schedule can be a challenge. You also have to be careful about letting them nap too late at times. As Jim Gaffigan explains in his book *Dad Is Fat,* a nap for some toddlers can be a payday loan that you will pay for when bedtime comes, and bedtime is an important window of quiet time for parents that you want to protect.

Screen time: Yes, everyone has opinions about how awful screens are, or they have stories of some unicorn toddler who can occupy themselves for hours playing with a stack of nesting cups. But sooner or later you will need a few moments of quiet, and the fastest way to get it is to put headphones on a child and let them watch something on a tablet. If your child is still at the age where wearing headphones is the equivalent of being asked to wear a headband made from porcupine quills, then proceed to the next step.

Noise canceling headphones: There will come a point in your life when your child attaches to a TV show with a character that has a grating voice, or your child decides their new favorite game is screaming as loud as they can. So get some noise canceling headphones for yourself. You can wear them to drown out noise so that you can focus on something other than the singing puppet on the TV. I was in a book club with another mom who said that she got most of her reading time in by sitting on the couch while wearing noise canceling headphones as her child watched TV. That was smart. Be like her.

Audiobooks: Once your kids are old enough to be engaged by stories, audiobooks are a good way to buy you some quiet time. They can listen to something semi-educational and you can focus on something else, like reading your own book in another room.

Get out of sight: If you try to open your laptop while sitting next to a toddler, the toddler will take that as an invitation to try to climb on your lap and slap the keyboard. So if you can remove yourself to an adjacent room where you can still see and hear your child, but they can't see you, do.

Hide the loud toys: Some well-meaning person or previously unidentified nemesis will buy your child a plastic instrument that will make you want to punch a wall every time you hear it. Your child will love the instrument and you will have visions of lighting it on fire and throwing it out the window. Save yourself the spectacle of a parent meltdown by just hiding those toys. Preferably in the trash can.

Invent some quiet contests: Hand out rewards for whoever can be quiet the longest or whisper all week. The child who wins or loses gets screen time.

MATH WORD PROBLEMS FOR PARENTS SEEKING QUIET TIME

- If your child normally takes a two-hour nap in the afternoon but fell asleep this morning for five minutes in the car, calculate the odds that they will still take a nap that day.
- Quinn's child is allowed to watch one 22-minute TV show in the afternoon after lunch. List 10 quiet things Quinn's dad can do in 22 minutes.

- Hector received a toy with a loud siren noise on it for his birthday. If Hector's dad hides all the batteries in the house, which will be worse—his toddler's meltdown or the sound of the siren noise on the toy?

- Maya's toddler gets out of bed approximately 10 times a night between the hours of 7 p.m. and 6 a.m. Estimate the number of moments that Maya's parents aren't cherishing each evening.

- If there were a toy that was guaranteed to keep your child occupied for at least an hour a day so you could concentrate on something else, calculate how much you would be willing to pay for it.

22

Bedtime Struggles

I have a friend who told me about a mom who lets her young kids stay up as late as they want during the summer because she likes all the energy of a busy house. I, on the other hand, purchased the darkest blackout shades possible when my kids were little so that even when the sun was shining brightly into the night in June, I could still trick them into sticking to their regular bedtime. I need the quiet time at the end of the day to restore my energy, and bedtime is like seeing a pot of gold positioned at the other end of a room. But there's a catch: I have to chase a Tasmanian devil through a ninja course to get to it.

After you've spent the day negotiating toddler feelings, making snacks, and having a small person hang all over you, then you are probably more than ready for some alone time. But bedtime with a toddler can be tough. You are exhausted and your child is also exhausted, but they behave like a cornered wild animal when you try to get them to change into their pajamas. Reading to your child can be a nice shared activity when you aren't exhausted (or your child has fever-induced lethargy), but reading to them at bedtime is daunting when it's been a long day. When I'm tired, sometimes I will try to cut down on reading at bedtime by letting my kids pick just one book. But then they will inevitably pick a book like *Richard Scarry's Cars and Trucks and Things That Go*. Do you know how many pages that book has? Seventy-two. Do you know how many illustrations and words are in that book? Approximately 1 million. I sometimes try to just read part of it or skip some words or pages, but my kids inevitably catch on and start insisting that I read "All the words." So learn from my mistakes and only keep short books in your kid's room for reading at bedtime.

COMMON BEDTIME PROBLEMS AND SOLUTIONS

- **Problem**: Child will not get into the bath.
  Solution: Buy 5,000 bath products to lure child into bath.
- **Problem**: Child will not get out of the bath.
  Solution: Promise them an extra story, a treat in the morning, or a pony if they will just get out of the bath.
- **Problem**: Child acts like a cat trying to be stuffed into a Halloween costume when you get near them with a toothbrush.
  Solution: Start saving money for dental work.

- **Problem**: Child wants you to make up a story.
  Solution: Digital device tells your child a bedtime story.
- **Problem**: Child wants you to read a picture book that is far too long for an exhausted parent at the end of the day.
  Solution: Read the book to the child one time and then make a mental note to hide the book somewhere and then gift it to a parenting nemesis.
- **Problem**: You have run out of patience and not behaved in a completely calm and chill manner at bedtime.
  Solution: Remember, your child's future therapist needs to make a living too.
- **Problem**: Child wants another drink of water.
  Solution: Install a toddler-size water feeder near their bed, like the ones used to feed hamsters.
- **Problem**: Child wants you to lie down with them until they fall asleep.
  Solution: Lie down, fall asleep, and wake up disoriented an hour later. Or just stay there for the rest of the night so you can get the child back in bed easily when they get up in the middle of the night.
- **Problem**: The time change for daylight savings time means your child is staying up an extra hour.
  Solution: Cry.

Children's Books Retitled for Bedtime

Goodnight Toy That Makes a Loud Boom

•

The Very Hungry Child at Bedtime

•

Don't Let the Toddler Get Out of Bed!

•

*Harold and the Purple Look on His Dad's Face When
Harold Got Out of Bed for the 20th Time That Night*

•

*Oh, the Places You'll Go, in Your Dreams When You
Fall Asleep*

•

*If You Give a Parent a Little Bit of Alone Time and
a Cookie, They Will Be in a Much Better Mood
in the Morning*

WHAT YOU'LL DO WITH YOUR ALONE TIME ONCE YOUR CHILD IS ACTUALLY ASLEEP

1. Plan to stay up for a just a little bit, but definitely be in bed by 10 p.m.
2. Turn on a marathon of *House Hunters* on HGTV.
3. Scroll social media while half watching the show.
4. Eat some snacks.
5. Get very invested in which house the couple moving to Oklahoma City will select. Decide that maybe you can stay up until 10:30 p.m.
6. Log on to your computer and respond to emails while the couple tours homes and are distraught over the lack of a double vanity in the fourth bathroom.

7. Somehow, it's 11 p.m. but you *must* stay up to know which tiny home the family of five on TV will select as their completely unrealistic future home.

8. Google divorce rates for people living in tiny homes.

9. Realize it's midnight and you need to go to bed, no matter how deep your need is to find out which apartment the couple moving to Belarus to pursue the boyfriend's dream of living abroad will select.

10. Finally go to bed. Plan to definitely go to bed by 10 p.m. tomorrow.

23

The Great Outdoors: How to Survive the Playground

You probably did not spend a lot of time at your local playground prior to having children. But once you have young humans of your own, you will quickly locate any patch of green space within a 10-mile radius of your home. Parks and playgrounds are great destinations: They get you out of the house, plus they give your child a chance to be active and sustain injuries. The only problem is, you will hardly ever be the only people at the playground, so this means you will have to socialize with other parents and kids. When my first child was born, I took him to a nearby playground fairly frequently. Some kids would occasionally bring toy trucks or sand shovels and buckets and then leave them unattended near one of the play structures. Of course, my son would want to grab the toys and play with them—something I didn't want him to do without asking, because I had witnessed enough toddler toy battles to know how quickly things could turn into *The Real Housechildren of Playground City*. Even if the caregiver did say it was fine, sometimes the kid was not actually fine with another kid touching their sand bucket and would start crying or screaming. I would often try to just steer my son away from the toys, but he was attracted to them like any baby is to any object that can fit in their mouth. We tried bringing our own toys sometimes, but then we would just have the same problem in reverse. As a result, what was supposed to be a fairly stress-free outing would turn into a stressful situation in which I wished the toys had just stayed home.

When we moved to a different area after my second son was born, we found nearby parks with sandboxes where a bunch of community plastic trucks and sand buckets were left for anyone to play with. There would still be some fights over a particularly coveted dump truck, but at least no one could claim ownership of it. And on some amazing days, we would show up to a sandbox and no other kids would be there at all. The moral of the story being, if a social situation at a park is stressing you out, you can always move.

Even if you aren't dealing with the shared toy problem, there are a variety of kid and parent personalities at the playground that you will have to manage. Kids on the playground (including your own) will bite, cut the lines, and lick the handrails. And unlike child play classes, there is no adult playground facilitator to tell kids to follow some basic rules. Sometimes caregivers will enforce rules, and sometimes they won't. So there is always some chance that the playground will turn into *Lord of the Flies*.

IDEAL TIMES TO VISIT THE PLAYGROUND

During nap time: Play areas tend to thin out a little bit in the afternoon when many children nap, so you are likely to encounter fewer people at this time of day. If your child also naps at this time, you can just let them nap in the stroller while you enjoy some quiet time alone sitting on a bench at the park.

Early in the morning: Have a child who wakes at 5 a.m.? Time to head to the park.

During a blizzard: Most people don't go to the playground in a blizzard. But if they do, chances are they will be so bundled up in parkas and goggles that any small talk will just turn into indistinguishable muffled sounds.

During a heatwave: You and your child will be uncomfortable, but not for social reasons.

In the middle of the night: Do you have one of those kids who wakes up at 2 a.m. and refuses to go back to sleep? Now might be a good time to go push them on some swings.

Other Park Tips

- If you don't want to talk to other adults, just talk to your kid. Following them up to the top of the tallest play structure will work in a pinch.
- The swings are social. Pushing your child on a swing often positions you next to another caregiver doing the

same thing. So if you aren't in the mood to talk, install a swing set in your own backyard.

- Playgrounds get progressively easier as your kids get older and you aren't required to hold their hands while they walk up the stairs/push them on the swings/slide down the slides with them. A time is coming when you may be able to just sit for a bit.

TYPES OF CAREGIVERS YOU'LL ENCOUNTER AT THE PLAYGROUND

There are a variety of people at a playground. After you've visited a few hundred times, you'll start to recognize some of these types.

The Small Talker: This person will chat you up from the moment you arrive at the park until the moment you leave about topics that don't really interest you. If you are not in the mood to chat, try bringing a pair of binoculars in your stroller so that you can scope out the playground from a safe distance before arriving and make an abrupt course correction if need be. Just don't make the mistake of telling your child that you are going to the park before you leave, because their screams of protest when you decide to go somewhere else will be heard for miles.

The Games Parent: This parent (or grandparent) will be all-in on make-believe playground games. They will announce that the ground is lava and spend an hour pretending to be a lava monster and chasing their children around the play structures. Your child will gravitate to them because they are more enthusiastic and energetic than you are. The Games Parent will make you feel slightly bad that you don't have more energy, but mostly you'll feel good because your child can get in on that lava game while you scroll through your phone from the safety of a park bench.

The Super Nanny: This nanny will be caring for triplets and conversing with them in fluent French and German. You will be able to spot her because she will have the look of someone who has gotten eight hours of uninterrupted sleep. The kids in her charge are well-behaved and will always leave the playground when it's time to go without a meltdown. She will ask if you want to have a playdate sometime, but you will always find excuses because you don't want her to see how much you don't have your parenting act together.

The Hyper-Vigilant Parent: This parent will always be a few steps behind his child to make sure the kid doesn't topple over backward on the stairs or walk in front of a child on the swing. If you do this too, you might be able to bond with the parent over your discussion of the best baby gates and monitors to purchase. If you do not do this, you can probably hang back a bit—The Hyper-Vigilant Parent is probably also keeping an eye on your child.

The Glam Parent: This parent is basically the Posh Spice of the playground. She will have perfectly blown out hair and her kids will be wearing bespoke white rompers. Luckily, she will probably not try to talk to you because she will be on the phone scheduling her latest magazine cover shoot.

The Ultra Free-Range Parent: Their child will be the one sitting unattended on top of the swing structure. Luckily, you won't have to interact with Ultra Free-Range Parents at all because while their child is at the park the parents are back at their house.

The Disheveled Parent: This parent will always show up to the park with messy hair and wrinkled clothes. They will spend a lot of time trying to sit on a quiet bench on the sidelines. This parent may be your parenting friend soul mate. So try to say hi or tuck a note into their diaper bag asking if they want to meet at the park again sometime.

24

Food Fights: Eating Out with Your Toddler

The first time I went out to eat with a baby, I assumed the restaurant wouldn't be that crowded since we were having dinner at 5 p.m. Maybe there would be a few senior citizens and other parents at that hour, but not too many people who would roll their eyes when they saw a baby come in. But what I had failed to consider was happy hour. Early family dinner hour coincides with happy hour, which means there is a good possibility your child will throw a baby puff into the martini on a nearby table of carefree twentysomethings. (But on the upside, at least the happy hour attendees won't have paid that much for their martini.) One of the main stresses of taking small children out to eat is what other people are going to think about the audacity of you a) daring to have kids and b) thinking they should be allowed to go out in public before the age of 10. My eating-out-with-kids experiences have ranged from scowls from strangers to strangers seeming to be more excited to see my kids than me. A lot depends on the time and location for such meals, but the reactions from other clientele are like prizes from those cheap plastic egg toy surprise machines—you never know what you will get.

Toddlers in restaurants have launched a million social media rants with people staking their claims pretty firmly in the yes or no camp. This can make it anxiety-inducing to take a toddler to eat somewhere other than your house. Most parents who live in their own heads a lot try to strategize about when and where to bring a finicky two-year-old to eat. While some parent will inevitably claim their two-year-old can sit quietly at Le Bernardin and munch on sea urchin and sip from a glass goblet, most people know that the parent is just making stuff up to look impressive on social media. During the toddler years, you will probably do a lot of eating at home, but still, you may occasionally want to eat somewhere that doesn't feature an indoor slide. If your child has a meltdown, take comfort in the fact that this is not the first one the place has seen, and that the person scowling at you from the corner table probably threw plenty of meltdowns of their own when they were a child. Plus, your screaming toddler might grow up to be the surgeon that saves the life of the grumpy person seated next to you one day, so in 30 years, you'll really show them. One upside to a restaurant meltdown is that there is a solid chance that you will never see the people in the restaurant again after said occurrence. If you arrive at a restaurant with your toddler and spot someone you know in the dining area, it's best to just turn around and walk out.

UPSIDES AND DOWNSIDES OF OPTIONS FOR EATING OUT WITH SMALL CHILDREN

Fast Food Restaurants

Upside: Kids are pretty much expected and there are kid-friendly meals and play spaces, leading to less judgmental looks.

Downside: The kids play area can quickly turn into *The Hunger Games,* leading to the possibility you will need to intervene/have awkward conversations with other parents.

Upscale Order-at-the-Counter Restaurants and Food Halls

Upside: You can get some decent food and drinks and choose your own seating to be away from the people who seem to most dislike kids.

Downside: You have to carry a tray full of food and a kid to a table and there is a 50/50 chance something will fall on the ground.

Quick Sit-Down Restaurants

Upside: You get to sit down while food is brought to you, and some chain restaurants even provide tablets to entertain kids while waiting for food to arrive.

Downside: Hard to completely enjoy your food when you are concerned about other patrons who are judgy and may be inspired to pen a viral essay about how kids today don't know how to wait for a meal in a restaurant.

Fancy Sit-Down Restaurants

Upside: You get to post an impressive humblebrag to Instagram.

Downside: Your family may inspire a new "no kids under 12 years old allowed in the restaurant" policy that will be in place for years to come.

INSPIRATIONAL QUOTES FOR THE PARENT TAKING A TODDLER OUT TO EAT

- "You are never too old to set another goal, like only taking your child outside the restaurant to walk around three times instead of five while waiting for your breakfast to arrive."
- "Always look the world straight in the eye. Even if you are carrying a screaming child out of a restaurant."
- "Believe that the grimace on the woman at the table next to you is not about the noise that your kids are making but about something else, like how annoyingly her husband is chewing his food."

- "I am afraid of nothing. Not even the wine glass filled with water that the server just placed in front of my two-year-old."
- "Act as if what you do makes no difference. The meltdown would have happened regardless of whether or not one of the chips on your child's plate was broken."

FAMILY GATHERINGS

In addition to eating out, another challenge for the overthinking parent is the extended family meal gathering. You will probably need to visit a family member's home for a holiday or other special occasion several times when your child is young. Holidays can prove tricky because meals are often served at nontypical mealtimes, take longer than expected to be done, and may involve your toddler sitting next to Great-Uncle Gary, who thinks children should be seen and not heard. While you can always skip going out to a restaurant if your child misses a nap, it's harder to skip Thanksgiving dinner. Some things that might help:

- **Host at your house:** If you host the event, then you will need to cook and clean, but you will also get to set the time, choose some of the food being served, and your child can still take a nap in their own room if they need one.
- **Make requests of the host:** If you are going to a relative's house, then try to lobby for a time, foods, and a table setup that will work better for young kids. If they are inflexible on these things, just bring your toddler to

a meal during nap time and they won't make the same mistake again.

- **Remind yourself about relative amnesia:** Some people's kids probably didn't behave as well as they think they did, and you'll just have to pretend you don't hear the negative comments in the same way that you've been pretending for years to not hear all the comments about politics during holiday gatherings.

THE HUNGER GAMES GLOSSARY FOR EATING OUTSIDE THE HOUSE WITH A TODDLER

Eating outside the house with a toddler may make you feel like you've been dropped into the dystopian universe of *The Hunger Games.* Indeed, a few lines from those books seem prescient:

Quote: "I volunteer as tribute."
   Translation: *I will tell the child that this place doesn't have waffle fries.*

Quote: "Happy Hunger Games!"
   Translation: *"Happy Thanksgiving!"*

Quote: "And may the odds be ever in your favor."
   Translation: *Hope no one with a smartphone records your child's meltdown today.*

Quote: "Destroying things is much easier than making them."

Translation: *If you leave the heirloom gravy boat near the child, it will be shattered by the end of the meal.*

Quote: "I don't want to lose the boy with the bread."

Translation: *Your toddler just grabbed the breadbasket and is running toward the door.*

Quote: "You here to finish me off, Sweetheart?"

Translation: *A judgy parent from preschool is sitting at the next table.*

Quote: "Here's some advice. Stay alive."

Translation: *A relative's birthday dinner has just been reserved at a fancy restaurant.*

Quote: "Hope is the only thing stronger than fear."

Translation: *I hope they will have childproof tableware.*

Quote: "Katniss, the girl who was on fire!"

Translation: *Be careful, those candles on the table are real.*

Quote: "Yes, frosting. The final defense of the dying."

Translation: *Your child just threw a piece of birthday cake at Great-Uncle Gary.*

Quote: "District 12: Where you can starve to death in safety."

Translation: *"Let's just stay in for dinner tonight."*

25

I Need You! Dealing with Constant Interruptions

Small children's attention spans are short, and they prefer to eat their "meals" spread out in 20 small portions throughout the day. They are also too young to get themselves a snack or a drink, go to the bathroom on their own, and sometimes they have more questions than an episode of *Jeopardy!* Since you are probably trying to accomplish other things while you're around them—like making dinner, paying bills, or reading a very important piece of celebrity gossip on social media—the constant interruptions can slowly chip away at any remaining levels of patience that you have. And if you are the type of person who likes to have time and space to concentrate on something, you may not take the constant interruptions with the grace of a 1950s TV mom. Looking for a way to carve out some time so you can concentrate on something important like creating the ideal toy organization system or solving a murder mystery? Here are some ideas to cope:

Get someone else to watch your kid. When my kids were young, I worked from home a couple of days a week and my kids went to day care the other days. I could manage work from home better when I only had one child, but once I had two kids and no reliable nap time, I added more childcare days so I could have time to focus. Childcare is expensive and not always an option, of course. Getting a spouse or friend or family member to watch your kid for a while is an excellent stopgap solution. Having the time to concentrate on something for longer than five minutes can be a godsend, even if the thing you are concentrating on is just the latest lengthy fight over food additives in your online parenting group.

Don't feel guilty. Some parenting publications will tell you the problem is with you. You wouldn't get asked for a snack every five minutes if you only served children food at mealtimes and if a child refuses to eat dinner you should not give them any more food for the rest of the night. But what these advice-dispensers don't tell you is how to manage an overtired toddler who skipped dinner without you both ending up in tears. Just do what you have to do and don't feel guilty if that means throwing snack packs at your child several times a day.

Hide from your child. You won't have to answer a lot of questions about why cats have tails if your child can't find you. Just don't leave your child near any cats while you are hiding.

Learn how to handle interruptions with grace and without ever getting frustrated. When you figure out how to do this, let me know.

HOW TO CHECK YOUR EMAIL WHILE WATCHING A TODDLER

1. Turn on a TV show for your toddler. No, not that super educational one that claims to teach her to read. Look for a show she can really concentrate on, something with princesses or ninjas or periodic loud *BOING* sound effects.
2. Put child in front of said show with a bowl of crackers and a drink.
3. Sit on the couch and open laptop.
4. Watch child spill crackers on the couch.
5. Clean up crackers and get a new serving of them in special container with spill-proof lid.
6. Sit back down and open laptop. Wait for computer to turn on.
7. Child asks for more crackers.
8. Get more crackers and return to couch and laptop. Open browser and type address for your email.
9. Child wants you to watch hilarious talking donkey on the show.
10. Feign interest in talking donkey for a minute and then return your attention back to your screen.
11. Toddler comes over to you and starts treating your keyboard like it's a broken buzzer on a game show.

12. Remind child of hilarious donkey on the show. What is the donkey doing now? A dance that teaches children about life on the farm? Amazing! Child watches for a minute and then comes back to your keyboard and tries to get her cracker-covered hands on it.

13. Wipe child's hands, open blank document, and let her type for a couple of minutes. Return child's attention back to the show.

14. Child watches for another minute and then tries to climb on your lap.

15. Retrieve toy computer that you bought for child because some parent said that their toddler works happily and quietly beside them for hours when given a toy laptop.

16. Give child toy laptop. Watch child throw it onto the floor.

17. Change show to something new to try to capture child's attention for just a few more minutes. It's a commercial for a product your child will start asking for five times a day, every day, for the next two weeks. Perfect! Child starts watching.

18. Get into your email program and read the first sentence of one email before child asks for another snack. Give up, close the laptop, and go retrieve another snack and get your smartphone.

19. Sit down with smartphone and read the first half of one email before your child grabs the phone and takes off running for her room.

26

Babes in Travel Land: Traveling with Young Kids

When my first child was about seven months old, my husband and I took him on a trip to Florida with extended family, which meant his first plane ride. Babies on planes rival toddlers in restaurants as some of the most feared scenarios for parents and strangers alike. Some parents on planes have offered to buy drinks for the people seated near them if a baby cries or even gift goody bags and issue apology notes to other passengers when they board. This practice has led to a rash of think pieces about why parents shouldn't need to apologize for their child's existence. Given all the debate about babies on planes, I was anxious about my first plane ride with a baby. So as Murphy's Law would have it, my first plane ride with a baby was kind of a nightmare.

Things started out smoothly—we boarded the plane,

pulled away from the gate, and then the plane abruptly stopped on the tarmac because of a mechanical problem. We sat on the plane, unable to unbuckle our seatbelts or get up, while my son, who was overdue for a nap, started crying and didn't stop. We could not do any of the recommended shushing or swinging to try to get him to sleep, and while he previously had taken a pacifier, he apparently decided to celebrate his first plane ride by suddenly refusing one. At one point, the flight attendant volunteered to walk him up and down the plane for a while, which we were happy to let her do, and during the entire time an older gentleman seated next to us looked intently out the window, probably pretending he was on a very quiet deserted island. Eventually, we returned to the gate, got off the plane, and then waited for another plane to come in that we could board. A couple of hours later we boarded another plane and got back in the same seats with the same people who I'm sure were very excited to see us and our baby again.

After surviving the plane ride, we arrived at our rental house near the beach. Almost immediately we were hit with the reality of vacationing with a baby. My son ate scoops of sand by the handful and continued his home tendency to not nap for more than 30 minutes at a time. At some point midtrip, while we were frustratingly pushing our son on the beach in a stroller to try to get him to nap, my husband declared, "We're never taking another trip again." This seemed like a good plan to me at the time. Of course, we did end up taking other trips with small kids, and at some point on the trips we would often jokingly or not-so-jokingly declare we were never taking another trip again. Every trip with small kids was always loaded with the dangerous possibility of being the last! Still, being at home day after day with tiny humans is exhausting, and feeling like you can get away from it in some way, shape, or form is still alluring. You won't be sitting on a beach and sipping a cocktail while reading the latest summer best-seller, but you will at least get a change of scenery.

Luckily, if you are the type of person who tends to worry and overplan, you will probably spend a lot of time scouring family travel prep articles and arrive at your destination pretty well prepared for a variety of scenarios. There is also some sort of strange unspoken bond that you form with other parents who are also traveling with babies or small kids. You recognize that at least you aren't the only one on the plane with a crying baby, and so you smile and nod knowingly at them when you board. Airlines that allow you to choose your own seating also allow families to take over a whole section of the plane where they can sit in peace by forming a small parenting plane-survival community (except for a few twentysomethings who overslept and came late and will never make that mistake again).

SOCIAL CONSIDERATIONS WHEN TRAVELING WITH SMALL KIDS

Travel companions: Traveling with friends or family members can mean extra help, but it can also mean more socializing and the management of different schedules and opinions. So before agreeing to go on a joint vacation with friends or family, think about whether they are going to want you to bring your baby to eat dinner at a restaurant sometime after 5 p.m.

Lodging: Will you be sharing walls with other travelers who will hear your child throw their Duplo set against the wall? Is there a house rental somewhere in the middle of a remote, but not scary, dense forest?

Food: Are there kid-friendly places where you can go out to eat at your destination? Is there somewhere you can cook the only type of macaroni your child will eat?

Time zones: The idea of taking a small child on that beach vacation may sound nice until you realize that their internal alarm clocks are hard-set to wake up at 4 a.m. local time.

Activities: Can you take your kids to a destination that doesn't involve you having to make small talk with a bunch of strangers on a minibus headed to a cultural attraction that your child will throw a tantrum at?

PROS AND CONS OF DIFFERENT TRAVEL METHODS

Car Trips

Pro: You can bring a lot of stuff and you won't need to worry about subjecting those outside your car to your child's vehicular meltdowns.

Con: The drive can take a long time and some kids can't

stay in their car seats for more than 30 minutes without turning into wild wolverines.

Train Trips

Pro: Kids have some more freedom to move around and you can buy snacks if you forget to pack them.
Con: Other passengers may not be amused by your child driving a Thomas the Tank Engine over the tops of their heads.

Boat Trips

Pro: Kids may spend some of the trip being distracted by the sea.
Con: Kids may spend some of the trip throwing up into the sea.

Plane Trips

Pro: Very little judgment from others when you keep your child happy by letting them eat lollipops and play screens the entire time.
Con: Approximately 50 percent of plane passengers will scowl at you when they see you get on board with a small child, and they will really hate you if your child kicks their seat.

Walking Trips

Pro: Affordable and there's no need to pack that much as you will just walk around your neighborhood for a little bit and pretend you are on an actual vacation.

Con: Not actually a trip at all.

"WOULD-YOU-RATHERS" FOR PARENTS TRAVELING WITH KIDS

- Would you rather your child cry for five minutes on a crowded plane or for two hours in a car that only contains your family?
- Would you rather the parent seated next to you on a plane tell you about the meltdown their baby had on a plane 10 years ago or have them buy you an in-flight cocktail?
- Would you rather be sharing a hotel room wall with another family with crying kids or with a room full of people partying with loud music?
- Would you rather have your baby sleep through an entire flight while a stranger chats you up or have your baby wake up and cry so you don't have to make small talk?
- Would you rather your child has a meltdown on a train around strangers you'll never see again or relatives who will remember and continue to mention it for the next several years?
- Would you rather have to change your child's diaper in a rest stop bathroom or an airplane bathroom?

- When beginning a four-hour plane ride, would you rather your child either kick the seat of a person in front of you or loudly ask why the person across from you has weird hair?
- Would you rather have room service bring you a cocktail or just stay home and make your own cocktail?

27

Welcome to the Jungle: Starting Preschool

When your child enters preschool, you may have mixed feelings—on the one hand, you'll be getting more alone time! On the other hand, you'll need to interface with a variety of teachers, parents, and all-school gatherings. Entering the world of preschool requires that you navigate an entirely new set of social circumstances. Your parenting is often on full display during preschool drop-off and pickup, and if your child has a meltdown in the front of the school because you didn't let them eat a bag of gummy treats on the way there, plenty of teachers and parents will be able to witness it. If you do go ahead and let them have the gummies just so you can get them to school drop-off on time, then you will worry about the judgement other parents will throw at you for giving your child dental-danger candy before 8 a.m. What's more, your child is probably reporting all sorts of out-of-context things to their teachers and friends that you can overthink. Will your child tell your teacher that you said "shit" this weekend? Yes, probably.

When I was looking for preschools, I talked to another mom in my neighborhood who liked a local school. It had experienced educators and low student-to-staff ratios, and it wasn't too far from our house. It was starting to sound like a good contender until she mentioned the word *co-op*. I knew I wasn't up for spending a required amount of hours per month doing various jobs around the school—I could sign up for one-off volunteer things when my time allowed for it, but adding a lot of additional responsibilities on top of work and parenting sounded overwhelming. I realized that when looking for preschools, in addition to important things like educational styles and safety procedures, I needed to consider how social the school was.

PRESCHOOL SOCIALIZING CONSIDERATIONS

Are you required to be on a committee? Some schools want you to be involved in committees and planning, and other schools are happy to leave you alone. I think you know which one to choose.

Can you email or text the school when your child is home sick, or do you have to call? Don't subject yourself to more phone calls than necessary.

How many social events per year will they have? Is there a weekly parent participation event that you're supposed to go to? You may think that you can just skip those when you don't feel like going, but your kid may have other plans.

What is the policy on birthday parties? Some schools require students to invite all the kids in a class to a birthday party or have some other elaborate in-class celebration. If your child is also an introvert, they may not want to don a crown and do a dance on a table in front of the entire class. If they are an extrovert, then this sort of thing may be fine.

Is there a career day? Will you be required to show up and talk about what you do at some point? Do you do something that is less like data entry and more like rescuing people from burning buildings? If not, then start thinking about ways to make data entry exciting to preschoolers now.

Are you required to volunteer? And if so, for how many hours and what are the types of volunteer positions available? See the following list to identify the types of positions that might be right for you.

IDEAL VOLUNTEER POSITIONS FOR THE INTROVERTED PARENT

- Anything that involves making copies alone in a quiet room
- The person who reads books one-on-one with kids
- The person who buys tissue boxes in bulk and drops them off at the school

- Preschool librarian assistant
- The person who sends the electronic sign-up sheet for what to bring to the school picnic
- The person who sets up for the school picnic before anyone else arrives
- The person who bakes brownies for the school picnic, drops them off, and then eats dinner at home

Awkward Socializing at Preschool Bingo

Starting school will inevitably bring some awkward social moments. So, take a break from stressing out about preschool by playing this fun game. Reward yourself with whatever you want when you get bingo!

Said something awkward to child's teacher.	Thought about something awkward that you said to child's teacher six months ago.	Avoided making small talk with another parent.	Your child made small talk, so you didn't have to.	Conversed with another parent who you have something in common with.
Successfully avoided school book fair salesperson.	Your child had a meltdown at drop-off.	Your child had a meltdown at pickup.	Another child had a meltdown, thus making you feel better about yours.	Left rambling, incoherent message on school voice mail.
Remembered to brush your hair before drop-off.	Remembered to brush your child's hair before drop-off.	FREE SPACE	Realized your child isn't the class biter (yet).	Convinced your child not to invite entire class to birthday party.
Realized you will be out of town on the day of an all-class birthday party.	Child insisted on wearing Halloween costume to school in January.	RSVP'd to school event without ever having to make phone call.	Awkward silence at school social event.	Survived school social event.
Panicked at drop-off and commented on the weather to the teacher.	Avoided eye contact with extroverted parent.	Your child told the teacher at their Montessori school that they watched TV all weekend.	Survived parent-teacher conference.	Quiet moment alone while your child is at preschool.

28

The More the Scarier: Expecting Another Child

Just when you start to get the hang of the parenting thing, some people make the decision to throw a wrench in the process by having another kid. I was one of those people. I had my second son when my first one was about two and a half. In some ways, having a second kid wasn't as difficult as having the first because I was already semi-used to the sleep deprivation and lack of alone time, but in other ways it got harder. While pregnant with my first child, I spent a lot of time napping, going to prenatal yoga, and browsing Etsy stores for the exact right print to hang in the carefully decorated nursery. While pregnant with my second son, a lot of my outings now included a toddler, and I had to periodically take a break from playing with him to run in the bathroom and throw up. Here are some changes to prepare for when you have more than one kid:

Things get louder: With multiple kids there is twice the chance that a child is awake or having a meltdown over their food being too red at any given moment.

There is a lot more stuff: Twice the kids means twice the clothes/snacks/loud birthday party gift toys that will need to be silently disposed of in the dead of the night.

Alone time is scarcer: When I only had one kid, I found it easier to trade off with my husband to get alone time. Having a second child, particularly while one depended on me for breastfeeding, meant trading off was more difficult. If you are a single parent, getting a friend or sitter to cover multiple kids can be a more tricky and expensive negotiation. Alone time during nap time can also go out the window as siblings are born with an innate ability to not align their nap times.

Welcome to the sibling fight club: Before having another kid, I think I had some vision of it being easier because the kids would entertain each other. I probably got this idea from parents with amnesia about how their kids really behaved, or those parents who had some sort of unicorn children who never get jealous or had the urge to throw a truck at their sibling's head. My kids do sometimes play together, but they've also been known to fight over who gets to use the handheld vacuum cleaner. The jealousy thing also came out when my second child was a baby and my first was a toddler, which made things like feeding the baby more exhausting to negotiate. Still, I think they will eventually be able to entertain each other for hours each day, probably around the time they leave for college.

WAYS TO COPE

Bribery: Your oldest child may now be at the stage when they can accept treats as rewards for getting their own snack or not saying the baby should be sent back to the hospital again. Plenty of experts say that bribery and rewards are awful, but luckily there are other experts who say that rewards are a legitimate motivational strategy for some kids. So just remember, you can basically do whatever you want.

Childcare: Find an additional family member, babysitter, or extremely engaging tablet app to entertain your child.

Vacation: Volunteer for a work trip or arrange your own child-free parent-cation to get some time when you can sleep past 6 a.m. and small humans are not attached to or crawling all over you every minute of the day. The locale need not be far—a hotel near your house or a tent in your backyard will work.

FANTASIES FOR PARENTS OF YOUNG KIDS

- The children awake at their normal time of 5:30 a.m., but they play quietly in their crib/room and let you sleep until 6:15 a.m.
- Each day your toddler quietly plays with a special basket of books and toys while you breastfeed the baby, even though breastfeeding the baby occupies approximately 70 percent of your time each day and people who give this advice seem to lack some understanding of basic math skills and toddler behaviors.

- Your toddler gets a new wooden toy mallet set and uses it to pound pegs instead of her baby sister.
- All your kids are asleep by 8 p.m. and you're somehow able to stay awake until 9:30 p.m. You get to lie on the couch and watch a full half of a movie that came out sometime in the last five years.

29

Reflection Time

Congratulations! You've survived the first few years as a parent. Sure, you had to socialize with a lot of new people, but just think of how many awkward dinner parties that your baby got you out of. It may feel like you've actually been a parent for something like 10 years, because the early days of parenthood can seem extremely long. Or you may be thinking that "it goes so fast" because the early stages of parenting amnesia have already started to set in.

Now that you have been a parent for a little while, it's time to reflect on how it has all gone. First, take a moment to congratulate yourself on everything you've done: operated on little sleep, survived the parenting advice Thunderdome, and kept one or more small humans alive for a few years. Want to tally up more accomplishments? Just fill out the below worksheet.

WORKSHEET FOR WAYS IN WHICH YOU ARE KILLING IT AS A PARENT

1. Calculate how many parenting-related phone calls you've successfully made in the past 36+ months:

   _____

2. Calculate how many other parents you've met in the time since you've become a parent:

   _____

3. Tally up how many of the following you've attended in the last couple of years:

   ____ Parent/child classes

   ____ Playdates

   ____ Kids' birthday parties

   ____ Pediatrician visits

4. Estimate how many parenting-related social media fights you've read since becoming a parent:

   _____

5. Describe a time in the last few years when you survived and maybe even enjoyed an event that you were dreading going to:

   _____

   _____

   _____

   _____

   _____

6. Think of a bad fictional parent and list all the ways you are better than that parent:

_____

_____

_____

_____

7. List some things in your pre-kid life that you used to spend time overthinking that you no longer do because you are too busy trying to keep a small human alive:

_____

_____

_____

_____

8. List all the cute and silly things your kid(s) have done in the last few years:

_____

_____

_____

_____

9. List the ways in which being an introvert has been a benefit for you as a parent:

_____

_____

_____

_____

Scoring: Give yourself 100 to 1,000 points for each completed answer and then tally up your score. Any score higher than one point means you can buy yourself some fancy chocolate or new tripped-out minivan.

WAYS TO CELEBRATE YOUR FIRST FEW YEARS OF BEING A PARENT

Being a parent for a few years is worth celebrating in your own way—you've probably experienced a range of new emotions like deep love and deep rage, and it is worth letting loose a bit. Here are some ideas:

Hire a babysitter: Nothing helps celebrate parenthood more than a night away from your kids.

Order a cake: Most good celebrations start with baked goods.

Anniversary gift: Buy yourself a gift to commemorate the number of years that you have been a parent:

- One year (Paper): A stack of new books.
- Two year (Cotton): An expensive piece of clothing that you purchase based on a reason other than how well it hides spit-up.
- Three year (Leather): New leather seats for your minivan.

Homemade Molotov cocktail: Write down some of your most difficult parenting moments on a piece of paper, put the paper in a bottle, and then pour a flammable liquid on it and light it on fire. You don't want any would-be parents to accidentally find the paper and be scared off.

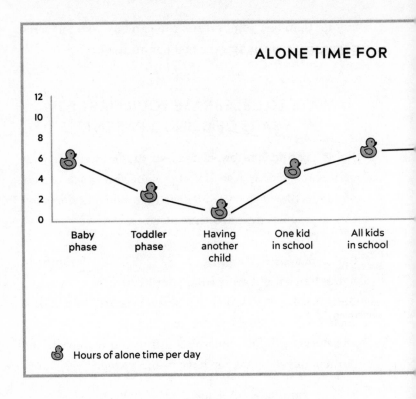

ALONE TIME FOR

Hours of alone time per day

Surgical celebration: Some people like to celebrate a milestone like this by doing something fun like getting a vasectomy or tubal ligation.

Huge, loud party including everyone you've met since becoming a parent: Ha! I meant a small gathering with your family and a few close friends with good food and drink. It's worth splurging a little, after all. Besides, you've probably been saving a lot of money by staying home all the time.

PARENTS OVER TIME

| Children old enough to be left in the car for 5 minutes while you run into the store to get something | Teen-age years | College years | When child moves back in with you after college | Children leave house again |

A FUTURE PLOT CHART FOR HOW YOUR ALONE TIME SHOULD NOW BE STEADILY INCREASING

Now that your kids are getting older, the good news is that there should be a lot more alone time on your horizon. In the coming years your kids should go to school, be able to play on their own more, and eventually even know how to pour themselves a glass of milk.

ACKNOWLEDGMENTS

First, I'd like to thank the random strangers who dispense parenting advice for giving me so much to write about. And to the handful of strangers who have stopped me on the street to say something positive about my parenting, thank you—you should definitely keep doing that for other parents.

Thanks to my agent, Saba Sulaiman, who believed in and championed this book from its early stages, and to my editor, Ann Treistman, and the entire team at The Countryman Press, who helped create and shape this book and get it out into the world.

Thanks to my parents, John and Regena, and sisters, Jennifer and Jessica, for supporting my writing from a young age and providing me with a wealth of useful parenting advice and help.

Thanks to all my writing feedback partners and friends over the years who have been so generous with revision notes and writing resources and especially to those who helped with this book at various stages. There are too many to name here, but you know who you are.

Thanks to my boys, Graham and Beck—without you, this book would not have been possible. Also, thanks to my husband, Dave, for your support and willingness to go on the introverted parenting journey with me.

And, finally, thanks to the makers of Minecraft for entertaining my children: You really helped to make writing a book while parenting during a pandemic possible.

INDEX

advice
  conflicting, 78–80
  managing others' opinions,
    16–17
  parenting amnesia, 62–63
  problems with common advice,
    74–75
  for quiet time, 140–42
  on sleep, 72, 74, 78
after the baby arrives, 57–58
alcohol, 11–13, 23
alone time, 73, 104–10, 147, 178–79,
  186–87
announcement options, 30–31
audiobooks, 141–42
awkward conversations, 18, 177

baby names, 41–48
  deliberation, 43–47
  places to look, 47–48
baby showers, 34–40
  after the party, 40
  games, 39–40
  the setup, 36–38
  top baby shower fears, 35
  virtual, 38–39
baby yoga, 114
bad sleepers, 72–73
bedtime, 144–48
  alone time, 147–48
  common problems and solutions,
    145–46
birth, 51–58
  after the baby arrives, 57–58
  birth plan, 54–56
  classes, 21–22
  labor, 52–54
birthday parties, 115–18
  attending, 127–32
  the basics, 116–17
  first birthday party theme ideas, 117–18
  pre-party options, 128–30
  survival prep list, 131–32
  survival strategies, 130
breastfeeding, 67–68
busybodies, 14

camouflaging your belly, 16
caregivers, 152–54
celebrating first few years, 185–87
cherishing parenting moments, 136–38
childcare, 90–98
classes
  baby prep classes, 20–21
  baby yoga, 114

birth classes, 21–22
  exercise, 19–20
  exit strategies, 114
  managing, 19–22
  music, 113
  parent-child, 111–14
  storytime, 114
  stroller exercise, 113
communication methods, 29–30, 103
conflicting advice, 78–79
connecting with other parents-to-be,
  24–25
coping with a second child, 180

doctor visits, 99–103
dreaded parenting task scorecard, 96

eating out, 155–61
evaluation criteria for visitors, 60–61
expecting another way, 24–27
  connecting to other parents-to-be,
    24–25
  invasive questions, 25–26
  self-care tips, 27
expecting a second child, 178–81

family gatherings, 159–60
fantasies for parents of young kids,
  180–81
fears about baby showers, 35
feeding your baby, 65–69
  breastfeeding, 67–68
  formula, 68–69
  motivational quotes, 69
first birthday parties, 117–18
first trimester, 11–14
  and alcohol, 11–13
  the busybody problem, 14
  and sickness, 13–14
first year, 51–118
  alone time, 104–10
  birthday parties, 115–18
  childcare, 90–98
  doctor visits, 99–103
  feeding your baby, 65–69
  information overload, 76–80
  parent friends, 81–89
  sleep, 70–75
  social overload, 59–64
formula feeding, 68–69
friends. *See* parent friends

games at baby showers, 39–40
good sleepers, 72
gross motor skills, 103

information overload, 76–80
    conflicting advice, 78–79
    parenting research headlines, 79–80
    social media, 77–78
interruptions, 162–65
introverted parents, ix–xiii, 84–86,
        102–3, 105, 175–76
invasive questions, 25–26

labor, 52–54
loud toys, 142

managing others' opinions, 16–17
mocktails for the parent-to-be, 23
motivational quotes, 69

naps, 140–41
noise, 139–43
noise canceling headphones, 141
nosy questions, 8–9

pandemic parenting, xiii
parental readiness challenges, 6–8
parent friends, 81–89
parent getaways, 108–10. *See also* alone
        time
parenting amnesia, 62–64
parenting discussion groups, 86–89
parenting research headlines, 79–80
parenting task scorecard, 96
park tips, 151–52
personal-social skills, 103
playdates, 121–26
    location considerations, 122–23
    potential problems and solutions,
        123–24
    screening questionnaire,
        125–26
playground, 149–54
pregnancy, 10–23
    alcohol, 11–13
    awkward conversations, 18
    baby prep classes, 20–21
    birth classes, 21–22
    camouflaging your belly, 16
    exercise classes, 19–20
    first trimester, 11–14
    managing classes, 19–22
    second trimester, 15–16
    sharing the news, 28–33
    sickness, 13–14
    third trimester, 16–22
preschool, 173–77
    bingo, 177
    socializing considerations,
        174–75
    volunteer positions, 175–76
problem solving, 103
public tantrums, 133–38

quiet time, 139–43

reflection, 182–87

screen time, 141
second children, 178–81
second trimester, 15–16
self-care tips, 27
setting up baby showers, 36–38
sharing the news, 28–33
    announcement options, 30–31
    communication methods, 29–30
    surprise option, 31–33
sickness during pregnancy, 13–14
sleep, 70–75
    advice, 72, 74, 78
    alone time, 73, 147–48
    bad sleepers, 72–73
    good sleepers, 72
    reasons why your baby isn't sleep-
        ing, 74–75
socializing at preschool, 174–75, 177
social media, 76–80
social overload, 59–64
    evaluation criteria for visitors, 60–61
    parenting amnesia, 62–64
    unwanted visitors, 61–62
storytime, 114
stroller exercise, 113

tantrums, 133–38
template for birth plan, 55–56
third trimester, 16–22
    awkward conversations, 18
    classes, 19–22
    managing others' opinions, 16–17
toddlers
    bedtime, 144–48
    birthday parties, 127–32
    eating out, 155–61
    interruptions, 162–65
    noise, 139–43
    playdates, 121–26
    the playground, 149–54
    preschool, 173–77
    tantrums, 133–38
    traveling, 166–72
traveling, 166–72
    boat trips, 170
    car trips, 169–70
    plane trips, 170
    and social considerations, 168–69
    train trips, 170
    walking trips, 171
    "would-you-rathers," 171–72

unwanted visitors, 61–62

virtual baby showers, 38–39
volunteer positions for the introverted
        parents, 175–76

worksheet of accomplishments, 183–85